Getting to the

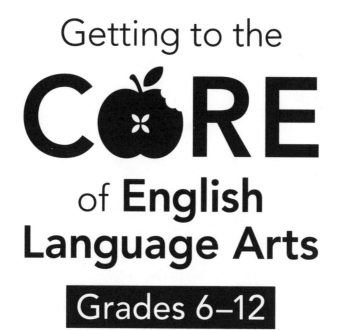

C**O**RE

of **English Language Arts**

Grades 6–12

This book is dedicated to my perfect husband, John, and three children, Emanuel, Anna, and Paul—for their love of knowledge and learning and for teaching me something new every day.

—Vicky

This book is dedicated to my grandfather, a book salesman, and my grandmother, an English teacher. They fostered in me a love of literature and the desire to teach.

—Maureen

Getting to the C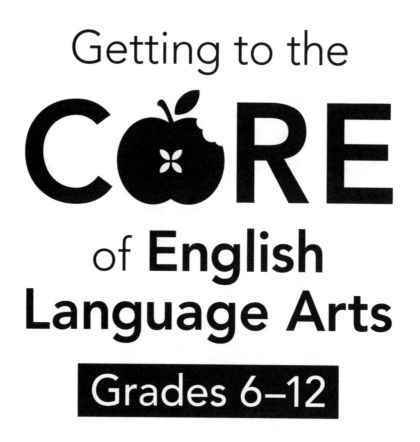RE

of English Language Arts

Grades 6–12

How to Meet the **Common Core State Standards** with Lessons from the Classroom

Vicky Giouroukakis
Maureen Connolly

Foreword by
Kenneth Lindblom

CORWIN
A SAGE Company

CORWIN
A SAGE Company

FOR INFORMATION:

Corwin
A SAGE Company
2455 Teller Road
Thousand Oaks, California 91320
(800) 233-9936
www.corwin.com

SAGE Publications Ltd.
1 Oliver's Yard
55 City Road
London EC1Y 1SP
United Kingdom

SAGE Publications India Pvt. Ltd.
B 1/I 1 Mohan Cooperative Industrial Area
Mathura Road, New Delhi 110 044
India

SAGE Publications Asia-Pacific Pte. Ltd.
3 Church Street
#10-04 Samsung Hub
Singapore 049483

Acquisitions Editor: Carol Chambers Collins
Associate Editor: Megan Bedell
Editorial Assistant: Sarah Bartlett
Production Editor: Amy Schroller
Copy Editor: Amy Rosenstein
Typesetter: C&M Digitals (P) Ltd.
Proofreader: Theresa Kay
Indexer: Judy Hunt
Cover Designer: Gail Buschman
Permissions Editor: Adele Hutchinson

Copyright © 2012 by Corwin

Printed in the United States of America

Library of Congress Cataloging-in-Publication Data

Giouroukakis, Vicky.
Getting to the core of English language arts, grades 6–12 : how to meet the common core state standards with lessons from the classroom / Vicky Giouroukakis, Maureen Connolly; Foreword by Kenneth Lindblom.

p. cm.
Includes bibliographical references and index.

ISBN 978-1-4522-1881-6 (pbk.)

1. Language arts (Secondary)—Curricula—United States—States. 2. Language arts (Secondary)—Standards—United States—States. I. Connolly, Maureen. II. Title.

LB1631.G48 2012
428.0071'2—dc23   2012008931

This book is printed on acid-free paper.

SUSTAINABLE FORESTRY INITIATIVE
Certified Chain of Custody
Promoting Sustainable Forestry
www.sfiprogram.org
SFI-01268
SFI label applies to text stock

13 14 15 16 10 9 8 7 6 5 4 3

Contents

Additional materials and resources related to
Getting to the Core of English Language Arts, Grades 6–12
can be found at http://www.corwin.com/ela6-12

Foreword

Every few years, teachers are given a new set of standards that will supposedly revolutionize how we deliver curriculum and improve students' development of the knowledge and skills needed to thrive in whatever the next era's challenges are. New standards typically point out what their promulgators describe as the failings of teachers and students, and they promise once and for all to set things right. Seasoned educators have seen this before. The Common Core State Standards (CCSS) are the latest iteration.

Although the CCSS are similar to previous standards in many ways, there is something that makes them different: Because they and the promised assessments have been adopted by nearly every state in the union, the CCSS bring us closer than ever to a standardized, national curriculum. The inertia behind the new standards is powerful. The financial and political backing the CCSS has received is significant. There is also considerable debate among educators regarding the overall value of these new standards, and there is a palpable sense of dissatisfaction regarding the manner in which the standards were developed, particularly the limited input educators were allowed.

Chances are your state has already adopted the CCSS and has embraced its promise to prompt curricula that will make students "college and career ready," a phrase that has become the CCSS mantra. Many veteran English teachers may be wearied from the promises of previous educational reforms, and they may need inspiration to embrace new standards now. Many new teachers look with trepidation upon the intricate dictates of the CCSS and wonder what in the world these standards might look like in real classrooms with real students. Like it or not, teachers will be expected to become well versed in the CCSS document. Unfortunately, the minutely detailed list of standards is every bit as engaging as your favorite phone book. But there is hope.

Enter Vicky Giouroukakis and Maureen Connolly.

I did not know Vicky and Maureen before I read *Getting to the Core of English Language Arts, Grades 6–12: How to Meet the Common Core State Standards with Lessons from the Classroom*. In reading their helpful, in-depth guide to CCSS, however, I feel as though I've made friends with two very knowledgeable, positive, and wise colleagues. Part guidebook, part pep talk, and part advice column, *Getting to the Core* takes the most important findings of the CCSS and shows teachers—veteran and new—how they can use the findings to help their students become "college and career ready."

Especially helpful is the introductory section, in which the authors overview the Common Core State Standards and tease out for busy teachers some of their most significant areas of focus; they also point out what they find to be the benefits of the new standards for students' literacy skills. Vicky and Maureen want teachers to learn to appreciate—as they clearly have—what the CCSS have to offer, to use the new standards to hone the excellent teaching they already do, and to enhance their teaching with new ideas inspired by the CCSS. I especially appreciate that the authors point out right away that teachers aren't necessarily required to create new lessons to comply with Common Core State Standards; much of the work good teachers already do will meet CCSS.

Following the introduction, the book is broken into four sections, each dealing with a major strand from the CCSS Anchor Standards—Reading, Writing, Speaking and Listening, and Language—and it concludes with a special focus on collaboration, something the book's coauthors know about. Teachers will find engaging, creative, CCSS-aligned lessons that make use of a variety of new and classic texts. One of the features of the book that makes it such an enjoyable read is a section before each lesson titled "Vicky and Maureen Speak" (or sometimes just Vicky or Maureen "speaks"). In these sections, the authors explain how they came up with the idea for the lesson and how it went with their own students. They describe how they may have adapted the lesson to fit CCSS and what tweaks they made after they tried it out with their students. Teachers will appreciate Vicky's and Maureen's substantial teaching experience, and these sections highlight nicely the kind of reflective practice they obviously employ in their own teaching.

Another helpful feature is the marginal sidebars. Throughout the book, readers will find "Tech Connection," "Theory Link," or "Differentiation Tip" sidebars that aim to highlight special elements or possible adaptations of the lessons. In this way, the book, as the authors put it, functions as an already-highlighted text. How could an Internet tool work with this writing assignment? Does this lesson fit with the philosophy of John Dewey, Benjamin Bloom, or Howard Gardner? Could this task be adapted for gifted or struggling students? The authors have wondered about these things, too, and they've included their thoughts about them.

The Common Core State Standards are here, and teachers and administrators will be expected to align curriculum to them and to the forthcoming standardized assessments. Although many of us would take issue with some of the standards, how they were produced, and what's left out of them, that doesn't mean we won't be expected to work with them. We're lucky to have two colleagues who've thought long and hard about the standards, found benefits for our students in them, and given us a useful, authoritative, and refreshingly readable guide to help us all get up to speed.

Kenneth Lindblom
Stony Brook University

Kenneth Lindblom is Associate Professor of English and Director of English Teacher Education at Stony Brook University. He began his career as an English teacher at

Columbia High School (East Greenbush, New York), and has taught writing and English at Syracuse University and Illinois State University. He is also editor of English Journal, *the 100-year-old, peer-reviewed journal for secondary and middle school English teachers published by the National Council of Teachers of English.*

Acknowledgments

We wish to acknowledge Corwin, and in particular Carol Chambers Collins, for their belief in our vision for this book and for their continued support of this product from start to finish. We would also like to thank our colleagues at our respective institutions of education—Molloy College and Mineola High School—for their sustained encouragement of our work, especially the English Language Arts professionals with whom we have worked over the years who have inspired us. In addition, we wish to express our gratitude to the students (both high school students and prospective teachers) we have taught in the past and will teach in the future for motivating us to become better teachers. Finally, we would like to sincerely thank those who work tirelessly to ensure quality education for all students.

A very special acknowledgment goes to our core families:

Vicky's core family: husband, John—my saint, for your uncommon and unwavering love, patience, and encouragement; Emanuel, Anna, and Paul—for showing me the true meaning of life and for your unconditional love and understanding; dad Polychronis and mom Constantina—for all the sacrifices you have made and still make for me and for fostering in me the values of family, education, and hard work; mom-in-law, Anna—for all your help and support; Steve, Elaine, Tina, Stephanie, Paul, and Peter; George, Margie, Tina, and Catherine—for your constant love.

Maureen's core family: mom, Elizabeth "Rose"—for always being eager to help; dad, John—for always being supportive of my education; Katie—for always being willing to listen; James—for always making me laugh; Rob—for always keeping me safe; Megan and Melissa—for always being eager to share a love of *Pinkalicious* reading and silly storytelling.

Publisher's Acknowledgments

Corwin gratefully acknowledges the contributions of the following reviewers:

Sandy Berka, English Teacher
Fond du Lac High School
Fond du Lac, WI

Lynn Frick, English Teacher
Sauk Prairie High School
Sauk City, WI

Jessica Gallo, Teacher, Ph.D. Student
    in Literacy Studies
Department of Curriculum and
    Instruction
University of Wisconsin–Madison
Madison, WI

Jan Mickler
National Literacy Project
Decatur, UT

Joanne E. Nelson, Instructional
    Resource Specialist, Social Studies
    and ELA
Brockton High School
Brockton, MA

Susan Stewart, Curriculum
    Consultant
Ashland University
Ashland, OH

Judith Sullivan, Supervisor, Office of
    Secondary English/LA
Baltimore County Public Schools
Baltimore, MD

Tracy N. Wilson
Reading Language Arts Coordinator
San Mateo County Office of
    Education
Redwood City, CA

Diana Yohe, Secondary ELA
    Program Planner
West Palm Beach, FL

About the Authors

Vicky Giouroukakis, PhD (née Vasiliki Menexas), is an Associate Professor in the Division of Education at Molloy College, Rockville Centre, New York. She teaches graduate courses to prospective and practicing secondary English teachers and English as a Second Language (ESL) teachers. Prior to her tenure at Molloy, Vicky taught English at a public high school in Queens, New York, and ESL to adolescents and adults. She also taught at Manhattanville College and Queens College, CUNY. Her research interests include adolescent literacy, standards and assessment, teacher education, and cultural and linguistic diversity. Her work has been featured in books and scholarly journals, and she frequently presents at regional, national, and international conferences. In 2010, Vicky was the recipient of the Educator of Excellence Award by the New York State English Council and has been serving on the Council's Executive Board since then. She has been interested in standards and assessment and how they affect teaching and learning ever since she began teaching. Moreover, her dissertation work was on the impact of state assessments in English on instructional practice. Vicky received a master's degree in English Education from Teachers College, Columbia University. She also earned a master's degree in TESOL and a doctorate in Reading/Writing/Literacy at the University of Pennsylvania. Vicky resides in New York with her supportive husband and three loving children. She can be reached by e-mail at vgiouroukakis@molloy.edu.

Maureen Connolly, EdD, has been an English teacher at Mineola High School on Long Island, New York, for 12 years. She has also worked as a professor of Education at Molloy College, Adelphi University, and Queens College. She has overseen service-learning grants for the New York Metropolitan Area and collaborated in the writing of several publications related to service-learning. While Maureen credits her passion for service to her mother, a music teacher who often coordinated trips for her pupils to perform at a local nursing home, she credits her love of literature and teaching to her grandmother, a professor of English at Hunter College, and her grandfather, a salesman for Macmillan. Maureen has developed many standards-based, service-learning projects that link community outreach, character education, and reading. In addition, she has been a part of the Learn to Serve with Character Research Project headed by New York State. Maureen earned her master's degree in Reading and her doctorate in Educational Leadership at St. John's University. She has been awarded the title of Honoree for the ASCD Outstanding Young Educator of the Year and granted the St. John's University LEAD Award. Also, she has presented workshops at regional, national, and international conferences, and volunteered to teach in India, Ghana, Peru, and Spain. Maureen is part of the Teachers for Global Classrooms Program which promotes global education. She believes that at the core of her profession is the need to develop purposeful learning that opens students' eyes to the potential for positive change in themselves and in their local, national, and global communities. Maureen resides in New York City and can be reached at mconnolly@mineola.k12.ny.us.

Introduction

How to Use This Book

As English teachers and teacher educators, we are flooded with books in our field about how to teach standards-based English Language Arts (ELA). As busy professionals, we are constantly sifting through these books, searching for the reader-friendly and practical works that will help us understand how to design standards-based lessons. This book is designed to help you, the ELA professional, become more familiar with the Common Core State Standards (CCSS) for ELA and to guide you in aligning your lesson plans with the CCSS. We get to the core of the state standards and uncover their benefits for the teaching of reading, writing, speaking and listening, and language. We provide lessons from the field for Grades 6–12 that guide students in meeting these standards. That said, we want to be clear that in order to meet the CCSS, you do not necessarily have to create brand-new lessons. Most of the examples that we include in this book are tried-and-true lessons that we have taught to actual students in actual classrooms over the past several years. Did we design these lessons with the CCSS in mind? The simple answer is *no*. However, we believe these lessons align with the CCSS because they include higher order thinking skills and varied levels of text complexity. In addition to lessons that we have developed and taught, we worked together to design new lessons or enhance preexisting lessons so as to meet the CCSS. We chose to do this because we wanted to model the experience of collaboration in planning and reflecting on our craft.

OVERVIEW OF CHAPTERS

In the first chapter of this book, we provide an overview of the CCSS for ELA and a rationale for their creation. Also, we include a discussion of best practices regarding lesson design. Our experience as high school teachers and as graduate education professors for preservice teachers has led us to value the Backward Design framework of Grant Wiggins and Jay McTighe. We also make clear the connection between the CCSS and the development of students' skills and knowledge by highlighting common verbs used (a) in the analysis of students' career and college readiness, (b) in the CCSS, and (c) by Bloom to designate higher order thinking. In addition, we discuss Gardner's theory of Multiple

Intelligences as a guide for your reflection on how meeting the CCSS helps you to address the needs of your students. We also discuss Dewey's concept of the productive citizen and the greater purpose that this concept gives to education.

CCSS OVERVIEW

The next four parts of the book include paired chapters based on the four strands of the CCSS: Reading, Writing, Speaking and Listening, and Language. In the first chapter within each pair, we discuss the CCSS for that particular strand in more depth and provide general descriptors of the expectations within that strand. It should be noted that the CCSS are based on College and Career Readiness (CCR) anchor standards. The following is an example of a CCR anchor standard within the Reading strand: *Read closely to determine what the text says explicitly and to make logical inferences from it; cite specific textual evidence when writing or speaking to support conclusions drawn from the text.* In order to streamline the language in our book, we consistently refer to the CCR anchor standards simply as *Anchor Standards.* We also focus on some of the Grade-Specific Standards, or expectations for that category according to grade level. These chapters are the ones whose titles begin with "The Benefits of CCSS for Teaching . . . . "

LESSONS

Lesson Format

In Chapters 3, 5, 7, and 9, we provide three sample lessons that are meant to serve as examples of CCSS-based lesson design. An introduction at the start of each applications chapter provides, for your consideration, some questions that we hope will make your reflection on lessons for that strand meaningful.

Before each lesson narrative, we include a template that outlines the workings of the lesson. This template includes the following:

1. Topic and Grade Level—ELA topic and grade levels 6–8, 9–10, or 11–12.

2. CCSS Strand—Reading, writing, speaking and listening, language.

3. Text Types and Purposes—The reading in which the students engage and/or the writing that students produce will fall under one of three CCSS categories: convey experience, argue/persuade, or explain/inform.

4. Timing—The expected number of class periods in which the lesson will take place, although this varies from class to class.

5. Backward Design Components of the Lesson—These include Desired Results/CCSS Addressed, Acceptable Evidence, and Learning Experiences and Instruction.

6. Teaching Strategies Utilized—These include guidance and monitoring, modeling, cooperative learning, discussion, and writing process.

7. Supplemental Resources—Additional resources for scaffolding instruction for students who may need support or expanding for students whose skills are advanced.

8. Technology/Media Opportunities—Ways of incorporating technology and media into the lesson.

9. Service Learning Link—Ways to tie student learning with outreach to the school, local, or global community.

10. Variations—Ways to modify or extend the lesson to meet the diverse needs of your student population. Variations also include opportunities for making interdisciplinary connections and incorporating additional or varied texts, skills, and instructional strategies.

This template is meant to serve as a preview of the lesson narrative and as a model for the analysis of your own lessons. We provide a blank copy of the same outline in the Appendix to serve as an organizer or checklist when you create new lessons.

Following the template is a lesson narrative. In each lesson narrative, we indicate, in brackets, the major CCSS for ELA that are addressed. Other CCSS are covered as well, but the major standards are those that the lesson addresses specifically. These lessons are not prescribed instruction; they are meant to be used as models and to be adapted to suit your particular students' needs. If you feel your students need to better develop their writing skills, please do not overlook the other three applications chapters. The skills within each lesson in this book are intertwined. For example, students' analysis of strong writing in the chapter "Reading Lessons From the Classroom" may help them develop as writers. The logical development of ideas called for in the Speaking and Listening chapter clearly also apply to the development of strong writing. The awareness of voice discussed in the Language chapter applies to effective writing as well.

Throughout the lesson narratives, you will also note the following marginal sidebars:

Tech Connection

Theory Link

Differentiation Tip

Tech Connections indicate how technology is incorporated into the lesson. Differentiation Tips help you to adapt your lessons based on your student population. Theory Links show how we believe the major, enduring theorists in education (Dewey, Bloom, and Gardner) would respond to the lesson.

Our purpose in presenting the lessons this way is to make your experience of reading through the lesson narratives similar to the experience of reading through a used book that has already been annotated. Some of the basic thinking is already done for you. The connections between the lessons and the CCSS are made overt. The marginal sidebars make technology infusion, differentiation, and theoretical connections explicit as well.

Based on some of the lessons presented in this book, samples of student work are posted at http://www.corwin.com/ela6-12. In the final chapter of this book, we focus on collaboration. We invite you to collaborate with *us* by submitting additional samples of student work that result from using this book. Our hope is that this sharing will start a dialogue regarding how to align the CCSS with the practicalities of our profession: lesson planning, teaching, and assessing student work.

Lesson Selection

When selecting lessons for this book, we sought to include both literary readings and informational readings. In addition, we wanted to present lessons that have clear opportunities for students to work independently to show what they have learned. According to the CCSS (NGA Center/CCSSO, 2010):

> Most of the required reading in college and workforce training programs is informational in structure and challenging in content; postsecondary education programs typically provide students with both a higher volume of such reading than is generally required in K–12 schools and comparatively little scaffolding. (p. 4)

The CCSS call for us to align with the National Assessment of Educational Progress (NAEP) requirement that a total of 70% of reading completed by secondary students be informational rather than literary by the time they reach 12th grade. This happens fairly naturally since the content areas outside of English include mainly informational reading. However, since students still think of their ELA classes as the place for developing their reading skills (even though they are reading in every subject area, including gym!), we felt it was important to include a balance of fiction- and nonfiction-based lessons in this book.

The majority of the lessons presented in this book include texts listed in Appendix B of the CCSS in ELA, which offers suggested texts for each grade-level strand. We included other texts that we felt are comparable to the suggested titles. In Chapter 2, we summarize the CCSS criteria for the recommended texts.

Because of the increased rigor outlined in the grade-specific standards, some lessons that we have taught in a high school setting are ideal for establishing knowledge at the 6–8 levels so that students enter ninth grade with a strong foundation for pursuing academic success. Just as the titles listed in Appendix B for the CCSS are *suggested* works, these lessons and the grade levels that we assign to them are also *suggested.* Our hope is that you will use our work as a springboard to develop your own lessons with texts that you deem ideal for your students.

In each applications chapter, we place an emphasis on students' communication skills (writing and speaking). The CCSS for ELA align with NAEP's 2011 Writing Framework, which requires 40% of student writing to be persuasive, 40% to be explanatory, and 20% to convey experience (real or imagined). Again, this is reasonable given the types of writing required of students in the content areas outside of ELA. However, to help you recognize how your ELA lessons support the development of writing style for each of these purposes, within this book is a reading lesson, a writing lesson, a speaking and listening lesson, and a language lesson that relates to the three CCSS designated text types and purposes: to convey experience, to explain/inform, and to argue/persuade (see Figure I.1).

Figure I.1 Lessons in This Book Organized by CCSS for ELA Strand, Grade Level, Assignment, and Text Types and Purposes

ELA Strand	Grade Level	Assignment	Text Types and Purposes
Reading	6–8	*Journey of the Sparrows* Graphic Novel Retelling	Convey Experience
	9–10	*Macbeth* Soliloquy	Explain/Inform
	11–12	Lincoln's Gettysburg Address	Argue/Persuade
Writing	6–8	Argument Rotation	Argue/Persuade
	9–10	Cyberbullying Letters	Explain/Inform
	11–12	*This American Life*	Convey Experience
Speaking and Listening	6–8	Life in a Bag	Convey Experience
	9–10	Editorial Videos	Argue/Persuade
	11–12	Show and Tell	Explain/Inform
Language	6–8	Literary Devices Booklet	Explain/Inform
	9–10	*Of Mice and Men* Visualization Exercise	Convey Experience
	11–12	Speech Analysis	Argue/Persuade

In Chapter, 3, on Reading, two lessons are based on works of fiction and one is based on a work of nonfiction. The reading skills needed to navigate the components of quality literature (higher order thinking, sophisticated vocabulary, universal themes) transfer to nonfiction or informational texts. In many of our lesson plans for the remaining three strands (Writing, Speaking/Listening, Language), we focus on nonfiction. In an article for the *School Library Journal,*

Marc Aronson (2008) bemoaned the fact that most high school students have not read an entire work of nonfiction from cover to cover:

> If we deny students the depth of understanding and analysis that nonfiction books provide, we leave them adrift on pop culture's superficial surface. And that means we've failed in our duty to offer kids the depth of thought and feeling that they wouldn't discover on their own. (para. 8)

Students need to see the application of literary elements/style to real-life stories and nonfiction documents. This awareness of the transfer of expression is one step in the journey that students may take as they model their writing, whether narrative or expository, after strong authors.

Collaboration

Throughout the lessons that we include in this book, you will recognize opportunities for the infusion of technology. Our students, digital natives, see technology as a necessity for effective communication. In the last chapter of this book, we will help you to navigate technology so as to "raise the roof" off of your school and collaborate with teachers in other buildings, other towns, other states, and other countries. You are not alone as you work to assist your students in meeting the CCSS. In fact, your support community is larger than ever thanks to technology, and this final chapter will help you to engage with your colleagues near and far.

Our hope is that this book will aid you in the development of a clearer understanding of the standards and how they affect instruction. We also hope that our lesson analysis will help you understand the key elements in CCSS-based ELA lessons and apply that understanding to the development of your own curriculum.

Laying the Foundation 1

An Overview

WHAT ARE THE CCSS IN ELA?

The fundamental importance of the Common Core State Standards (CCSS) for English Language Arts (ELA) is that for the first time in U.S. history, states are in agreement regarding what it means to be literate in the 21st century. Furthermore, the CCSS in ELA outline the literacy skills and understandings that students are expected to demonstrate in order to be college and career ready. Specifically, students read complex works of literature for comprehension and enjoyment; they read print and digital texts deeply and critically; they engage with high-quality literary and informational texts to broaden their knowledge base, experiences, and worldviews (National Governors Association Center for Best Practices [NGA Center]/Council of Chief State School Officers [CCSSO], 2010).

A consistent theme in school reform is the idea that our schools are failing because the standards are too low. The CCSS Initiative reflects recent efforts to establish an agreement on rigorous standards to measure what students should know. The focus on setting robust and uniform standards is familiar in the history of U.S. education. Even though uniform standard-setting can be traced back to the 19th century, it accelerated from the publication of *A Nation at Risk* in 1983, which reported low student achievement, low test scores, and a growing remediation in U.S. schools. It gained momentum with President Clinton's Goals 2000, which called for "a national crusade for education standards . . . representing what all our students must know to succeed in the knowledge economy of the twenty-first century" (1997, para. 26). In the same vein, the No Child Left Behind Act of 2001 called for high-quality assessments, instruction, and curriculum aligned with challenging standards "so that students, teachers, parents, and administrators can measure progress against common expectations for student academic achievement" (No Child Left Behind, 2002, para. 5).

We all know that there is no magic solution to the challenges of creating a rigorous, balanced, and fair system of education; however, the CCSS provide a framework for considerable improvement. These standards are the result of an effort coordinated by state leaders, including governors and state commissioners of education from 48 states, two territories, and the District of Columbia through membership in the NGA Center and the CCSSO "to provide a clear and consistent framework to prepare our children for college and the workforce" (NGA Center/CCSSO, 2010, "About the Standards," para. 1).

In the area of ELA, there are three sets of standards: (a) comprehensive standards for K–5; (b) ELA standards for 6–12; and (c) standards for 6–12 Literacy in History/Social Studies, Science, and Technical Subjects. This book will focus on the ELA standards for 6–12, which fall under the strands Reading, Writing, Speaking and Listening, and Language. In this book, we refer to Anchor Standards, general descriptors of expectations within each strand, by strand and number; in other words, R.6 means Reading, Anchor Standard 6.

The Reading Standards reflect the CCSS's great emphasis on reading of informational texts inside and outside of the ELA classroom. They consist of standards for reading literature and standards for informational texts (standards 1–9). They are aligned with the National Assessment of Educational Progress (NAEP) assessment framework in reading, which places greater attention on informational text (literary nonfiction). Reading standard 10 requires the reading of high-quality texts in a range of genres of increasing complexity.

The Writing Standards consist of three different types of writing: argument, explanatory, and narrative (standards 1–3). If instruction is to be aligned with the NAEP Writing Framework, the major focus of writing throughout high school should be on arguments and informative/explanatory texts (NGA Center/CCSSO, 2010).

The Speaking and Listening Standards focus on comprehension and collaboration (standards 1–3) in which students engage in purposeful informal and academic speaking and formal sharing of information and ideas in small and large group settings (standards 4–6).

Students who meet the Language Standards have knowledge of the conventions of standard English, and use standard English in formal writing and speaking as well as use language effectively. They also have knowledge of rich academic and content-specific vocabulary knowledge.

The CCSS Committees (NGA Center/CCSSO) made the groundbreaking and appropriate decision to establish standards for 6–12 Literacy in History/Social Studies, Science, and Technical Subjects that literacy experts have been advocating for decades. There is a proliferation of state-mandated courses on literacy in the content areas in teacher preparation programs. This interdisciplinary focus on literacy aligns with the CCSS literacy standards that put the responsibility of instructing students in reading and writing on teachers in all subject areas. In other words, teachers in math, science, social studies, and the technical subjects will need to teach the specialized language unique in their respective fields to enable students to comprehend the material. The CCSS in Literacy offer the promise of collaboration among teachers in different subjects, which can lead to seamless instruction. We will further discuss opportunities for collaboration in our final chapter.

HOW CAN WE USE BACKWARD DESIGN TO CREATE CCSS-BASED ELA CURRICULUM?

Backward Design (BD) is a curriculum design approach that is appropriate to use when trying to create standards-based ELA lessons because it relies on the essential ideas, like the standards, to serve as guiding principles for teaching and learning. It recognizes the centrality of standards and demonstrates how understanding is derived from and frames standards so that students can learn how to think and develop content knowledge and skills. BD also addresses the vastness of standards—as the knowledge base in content areas like science and history keeps increasing—by considering the "big ideas" in the content; these ideas are framed around "essential questions" to focus curriculum and instruction (Tomlinson & McTighe, 2006).

First introduced in 1998 and then revised and expanded by Grant Wiggins and Jay McTighe in 2005, BD (otherwise known as Understanding by Design, which is also the title of the book in which it is published) focuses first on goals that include standards and later on assessments and student learning experiences. The authors present the analogy of the road map to describe their approach: One needs to have a destination in mind first before planning the journey to successfully reach the end. Most teachers initially think about their teaching, what they will teach and how, without considering what student outcomes they want at the end of their instruction. In other words, they are concerned with inputs rather than outputs first. For example, they select a topic (persecution), then the text (*The Crucible*), followed by instructional methods (explicit instruction and cooperative learning), to help students meet the state standard (students will read for information and understanding). BD ensures that teachers identify first the standards that they want their students to meet, followed by student results called for by the standards, and then prepare learning activities that will lead to the desired results. "These standards provide a framework to help us identify teaching and learning priorities and guide our design of curriculum and assessments" (Wiggins & McTighe, 2001, pp. 7–8).

Because the content that needs to be covered is great, teachers need to make choices as to what standards and standards-based ideas to teach in order for students to gain *enduring understandings.* Enduring understandings go to the heart of the discipline and are the big ideas that we want students to retain in long-term memory after they have forgotten the details (Wiggins & McTighe, 2005). In his book *What's the Big Idea? Question-Driven Units to Motivate Reading, Writing, and Thinking,* Jim Burke (2010) ponders the use of the essential question to create enduring understandings:

> Perhaps my favorite and most useful question of all is, "What is the problem for which *x* is the solution?" This is a question that clarifies even as it challenges, helping me cut through the rationalizations that come so easily to so many of us as we are planning our classes. (pp. 23–24)

Wiggins and McTighe, along with Burke, encourage us to examine the value of our lessons by asking the following "big" questions: To what extent does the idea, topic, or process, having enduring value beyond the classroom, require uncovering, and offer the potential for engaging students (Wiggins & McTighe, 2005)? Are these big ideas applicable beyond the classroom to real life? Are they fruitful to examine and uncover? Do they provide opportunities to motivate students to learn?

Why BD?

Although most traditional curriculum planning relies on a linear process that is activity- and coverage-oriented (Wiggins & McTighe, 2005) without thoughtful consideration of student achievement, BD works the other way around; it is standards- and goals-oriented and focuses on student learning outcomes and achievement.

BD requires educators to first identify the end results (standards, goals), decide on what assessments will provide evidence of student learning called for by the standards, and then develop learning experiences and instruction that will enable students to achieve the desired results. Whereas traditional curriculum planning involves designing lessons before deciding what and how to teach, BD advocates the reverse—determining the achievement of desired learning before even planning learning experiences that will lead students to perform (Wiggins & McTighe, 2005). Standards, such as the CCSS, play the main role in BD and are the driving force of curriculum design and instructional planning. Teachers use the standards to help them think in terms of what learners should know and be able to do by the end of their instruction. According to Wiggins and McTighe (2005), teachers ask, What enduring understandings do we want students to gain from the lesson, curriculum unit, course, program of study that will have value beyond the classroom? What student learning needs—based on standards—can we identify, and then what instructional plan do we develop to meet those identified needs?

Description of BD

BD advocates a sequential planning that consists of three stages: (1) identify desired results, (2) determine acceptable evidence, and (3) plan learning experiences and instruction. In this section, we examine these three stages:

Stage 1: Identify desired results. In this first stage, educators consider their goals and establish curricular priorities. They ask themselves: What should students know and be able to do? What do I want them to understand as a result of my curriculum? What 21st century skills do I want them to acquire so that they may be successful in college, their careers, the world? This stage requires teachers to make choices about the content (topics), the important knowledge (facts, concepts), and skills (processes, strategies) that will be taught in the course or unit. In addition, they must determine what "enduring understandings" or "big ideas" they want students to retain long term and after the details are gone from their memory.

Stage 2: Determine acceptable evidence. The second stage focuses on what evidence will demonstrate that students have met the standards and desired results. The purpose of this stage is to ensure that students do not learn just content (facts and principles) but also acquire enduring, lifelong understanding. The evidence can be derived from a variety of assessment methods gathered over time that include formal and informal and formative and summative assessments, such as classroom observation, quizzes and tests, performance-based projects, and so forth.

Stage 3: Plan learning experiences and instruction. With the desired results and acceptable evidence determined, teachers are now ready to plan for learning experiences that will help students meet the standards and assessments. The planning will entail how to teach—what methods and resource materials to use—in a way that will provide students with the necessary knowledge and skills to achieve the desired results.

Application of BD to ELA Unit Design

In this section, we demonstrate the application of the three stages of BD with an example of a 3-week unit on bullying (for Grades 9–10) that aligns standards with curriculum and instruction (see Table 1.1). "Individual grade-specific standards can be identified by their strand, grade, and number" (NGA Center/CCSSO, 2010, p. 8), so that RL.9–10.1, for example, stands for Reading Literature, Grades 9–10, standard 1.

Stage 1: Identify desired results. We selected the three main CCSS grade-specific (9–10) standards (Reading, Writing, Speaking and Listening) that we would like to focus on in this unit:

Reading Standard: Key Ideas and Details

RL.9–10.1. Cite strong and thorough textual evidence to support analysis of what the text says explicitly as well as inferences drawn from the text.

Writing Standard: Research to Build and Present Knowledge

W.9–10.8. Gather relevant information from multiple authoritative print and digital sources, using advanced searches effectively; assess the usefulness of each source in answering the research question; integrate information into the text selectively to maintain the flow of ideas, avoiding plagiarism and following a standard format for citation.

Speaking and Listening Standard: Comprehension and Collaboration

SL.9–10.1. Initiate and participate effectively in a range of collaborative discussions (one-on-one, in groups, and teacher-led) with diverse partners on Grades 9–10 topics, texts, and issues, building on others' ideas and expressing their own clearly and persuasively.

Another thread that runs through all the CCSS and that is evident in this unit is multimodal learning/technology, which is a medium that enhances instruction and helps students reach the desired results.

We will use these standards as a foundation and develop the enduring understandings that we want our students to take away from this unit. We decide on the following enduring understandings:

- Students will understand essential concepts about bullying in literature and in real life.
- Students will understand how bullies evolve and how their actions impact other characters and events in a story and in real life.
- Students will understand their own behaviors and how they can take steps to prevent bullying from occurring.

These understandings are enduring because they are applied to real life, advance understanding beyond facts, and promote lifelong learning. Students will reflect on and examine the concept of bullying and how it relates to their own lives. They will explore ways in which they can prevent bullying from occurring.

This stage requires us to ask: What do we want students to know and be able to do as a result of this unit? We want them to know what bullying is and how it affects characters in literature and in real life. In terms of skills, we want them to be able to summarize and analyze key ideas and details about bullying in various literary and nonfiction texts (RL.1). In addition, they will have to perform a research project and gather relevant information from multiple sources, critique and analyze the sources, and integrate the information (W.8). Students will prepare for and participate effectively in a range of conversations and collaborations with diverse partners about the topic of bullying, building on others' ideas and expressing their own clearly and persuasively (SL.1).

In this stage, we need to examine the verbs in the standards that provide guidance for identifying knowledge and skills that students must acquire and for helping teachers develop assessments that measure student learning (Tomlinson & McTighe, 2006). For example, the verb phrases *participate effectively* and *exchange information* imply that a group presentation will be an appropriate assessment measure.

Stage 2: Determine acceptable evidence. The following task defines one form of assessment—performance task—used to demonstrate that students acquired the necessary understandings, knowledge, and skills.

> After discussing, reading, analyzing, and evaluating various texts (literary and nonfiction; print and digital) about bullying, the results of bullying (both legal and psychological), and steps that can be taken to prevent it, students will compose a letter to a preservice teacher containing an introduction briefly discussing how they are connected with cyberbullying, at least three startling facts from the class texts, and advice regarding steps that he or she

can take to help prevent bullying. The goal is to give sound advice to the preservice teacher to put a stop to bullying that negatively affects students.

The letter-writing performance task thoroughly provides the purpose of the lesson. It describes how the students will perform what is expected in the unit as well as an acceptable level of performance. An additional performance task will consist of a collaborative research project and presentation in which students work in groups to read and evaluate various print and Web sources on bullying and then present their findings to the whole class. This project will inform the composing of their letters to the preservice teachers as described above. Other assessments will include classroom observations, essay, journal writing, reader response entries, quizzes, and student self-evaluation rubrics.

Stage 3: Plan learning experiences and instruction. According to Wiggins and McTighe (2005), in this stage, we ask ourselves, What learning experiences and instruction will enable students to achieve the desired results? Some of the instructional activities of this unit will include the reading of a literary work that connects with the topic of bullying: *The Chocolate War* is one such example, but there are others, including *Animal Farm, The Cage, Macbeth,* and *Romeo and Juliet.* The theme among all of these works is that we should not accept injustice; we should take action. Students are given an avenue for creating change by writing letters to preservice teachers cautioning them about student bullying. In addition, students work in groups to examine information on bullying through sources such as articles, video of news broadcasts, and posts on websites. They evaluate these sources for credibility and present their findings to the whole group. This is an issue that students contend with on a daily basis, so all the instructional activities employed are motivating. In addition, technology and multimodal approaches (e.g., auditory, visual, digital) are employed as effective tools that will enhance and motivate student learning.

The instructional activities answer the often-heard student question of "Why do we have to read this?" by connecting the themes of the class readings with current social issues. It allows students to explore bullying as it may concern their peers and even themselves. The issue may directly relate to adolescents who can identify with being bullied or taunted or ostracized. It provides students with an authentic audience, therefore motivating them to polish their writing in a way that simply submitting to their teacher for a grade cannot. The teaching methods used to deliver sound content standards and foster positive learning experiences for students include cooperative learning, discussion, and teacher modeling.

BD is a curriculum design model that can be used to implement the CCSS because it focuses teachers specifically on the study of standards for the purpose of determining the goals of curricular units, specifying what knowledge and skills are important, and identifying acceptable evidence of understanding. It emphasizes standards-driven curriculum and speaks about the "how" and "why" to teach to promote student success.

Table 1.1   The Backward Design Approach Using the CCSS (Adapted from Wiggins & McTighe, 2005)

Key Design Questions	Responses
Stage 1. What are the desired results?	
(a) What CCSS for ELA does the unit address?	• Reading Standard: Key Ideas and Details [RL.9–10.1] • Writing Standard: Research to Build and Present Knowledge [W.9–10.8] • Speaking and Listening Standard: Comprehension and Collaboration [SL.9–10.1]
(b) What enduring understandings are desired?	• Students will understand essential concepts about bullying in literature. • Students will understand how bullies evolve and how their actions impact other characters and events in a story. • Students will apply their understanding of bullies to their own behaviors and how they can take steps to prevent bullying from occurring.
(c) What key knowledge and skills will students acquire as a result of this unit?	• Students will be able to interpret and analyze key ideas and details about bullying in various literary and nonfiction texts. • Students will be able to gather relevant information from multiple print and digital sources, assess the credibility and accuracy of each source, and integrate the information.
Stage 2. What is evidence of understanding?	
(a) Through what performance-based task will students demonstrate achievement of the desired results?	• Collaborative research project and presentation • Authentic letter writing
(b) Through what other evidence will students demonstrate achievement of the desired results?	• Observations • Essay • Reader response entries • Quizzes
(c) How will students reflect upon and assess their learning?	• Journals • Self-evaluation rubric
Stage 3. What learning experiences and instruction will enable students to achieve the desired results?	
(a) What learning experiences and teaching will promote student understanding, interest, and excellence?	• Reading and analysis of a literary work that connects with the topic of bullying • Research and evaluation of information about bullying; presentation of research findings • Letter writing

Key Design Questions	Responses
(b) What sources will be used to promote student understanding, interest, and excellence?	• Literary works: *The Chocolate War, Animal Farm, The Cage, Macbeth,* and *Romeo and Juliet* (print) • Newspaper articles (print and online) • Video of news broadcasts (video) • Posts on websites (online)
(c) What teaching methods will be employed to promote understanding, interest, and excellence?	• Cooperative learning • Discussion • Modeling

HOW DO THE CCSS AND BACKWARD DESIGN RELATE TO THE THEORIES OF DEWEY, BLOOM, AND GARDNER?

A clear connection can be made among BD, the CCSS, and the theories of John Dewey, Benjamin Bloom, and Howard Gardner. The ideas of these enduring educational theorists resonate in both the BD approach to curriculum planning and the CCSS that guide that planning. Dewey called for students to develop through experience into productive citizens. Bloom classified the different types of thinking—from simple recall to higher order skills like analysis and evaluation—required of all people in their journey toward good citizenry. Gardner recognized that just as the type of thinking required of students varies, the paths students take on that journey—their approach to developing skills and content knowledge—may vary as well.

Close to a century ago, John Dewey (1938) called for teachers to revise a system in which teachers imposed "adult standards, subject-matter, and methods on those who are only growing slowly toward maturity" (p. 18). His progressive approach to education was based on revealing a greater purpose for learning by connecting with life experience. Dewey asked, "What is the place and meaning of subject matter and of organization within experience?" (p. 20). When students understand the purpose of learning, they value that learning. Dewey explained, "The most important attitude that can be formed is that of the desire to go on learning" (p. 48). If students and teachers can agree upon the need to develop the skills outlined in the CCSS as purposeful, "enduring understandings" or "big ideas" that clearly have a place in today's world, then the topics addressed or the methods utilized can be adapted to fit students' needs and thereby fuel their desire to learn.

Certainly, the unit on bullying outlined above supports Dewey's call for education that has a clear purpose and that allows for student input. Students are learning about a topic that is relevant to their lives. They choose the articles (related to the topic) that have the most value to them. The assessment of their learning (letter to preservice teachers) is something that will help students make a positive change regarding this issue. We believe that these purposeful elements of this unit will inspire students to develop as thinkers and learners.

The types of thinking outlined in the CCSS are clearly in alignment with Benjamin Bloom's (1956) taxonomy of cognition. Verbs such as *synthesize, analyze,* and *evaluate* (bold in Table 1.2) and *cite, interpret, assess,* and *compare* (italicized in Table 1.2) are frequently found in the CCSS.

Table 1.2 Bloom's Taxonomy

Knowledge

Recognizing and recalling information

Action Verbs—*choose, cite, complete, define, describe, identify, indicate, list, locate, match, name, outline, recall, recognize, select, state*

Comprehension

Understanding the meaning of information

Action Verbs—*change, classify, convert, defend, describe, discuss, estimate, expand, explain, generalize, infer, interpret, paraphrase, predict, recognize, retell, summarize, translate*

Application

Using and applying information

Action Verbs—*apply, calculate, demonstrate, develop, discover, exhibit, modify, operate, participate, perform, plan, predict, relate, show, simulate, solve*

Analysis

Dissecting information into its component parts to comprehend the relationships

Action Verbs—*analyze, arrange, break down, categorize, classify, compare, contrast, debate, deduce, diagram, differentiate, discover, discriminate, group, identify, illustrate, inquire, organize, outline, relate, separate, subdivide*

Synthesis

Putting components together to generate new ideas

Action Verbs—*arrange, assemble, combine, compile, compose, constitute, create, design, develop, devise, document, explain, formulate, generate, hypothesize, imagine, invent, modify, organize, originate, plan, predict, produce, rearrange, reconstruct, revise, rewrite, synthesize, tell, transmit, write*

Evaluation

Judging the worth of information, an idea or opinion, a theory, thesis, or proposition

Action Verbs—*appraise, argue, assess, conclude, consider, criticize, decide, discriminate, estimate, evaluate, judge, justify, predict, rank, rate, recommend, relate, revise, standardize, support, validate*

Adapted from Dalton and Smith (1986, pp. 36–37).

We can see a variety of levels of thinking in the sample unit on bullying outlined earlier. Students are called to *understand* and interpret key concepts about bullying in literature (comprehension). They *apply* the lessons learned about bullying to their own lives (application). They *analyze* key ideas in readings about bullying (analysis). They *assess* the credibility of the sources (evaluation). They *integrate* the sources into a letter to preservice teachers (synthesis).

The CCSS for Reading (Grades 6–12) incorporate a range of sophistication in thinking. For example, "Key Ideas and Details" indicators begin at a simple level with verbs such as *read* and *cite*, but indicators 2 and 3 include more intensive expectations such as *determine* and *analyze*. Since different types of thinking are required of us as members of a productive society, different levels of cognition and ways of assessing each level make up acceptable evidence within well-developed CCSS-based lessons and units.

Howard Gardner (1983) examined the process that would lead students to desired end results regarding thinking and learning and determined that students need the flexibility to arrive at such results in their own way as well as options for how to provide evidence to support what they have learned. Table 1.3 lists Gardner's nine intelligences.

Table 1.3 Howard Gardner's Multiple Intelligences
1. **Visual-Spatial Intelligence**: The ability to think in images and represent internally the spatial world.
2. **Verbal-Linguistic Intelligence**:   The ability to use words and language.
3. **Logical-Mathematical Intelligence**: The ability to understand and use logic and numbers.
4. **Bodily-Kinesthetic Intelligence**: The ability to use one's body or control body movements to problem-solve or create something.
5. **Musical–Rhythmic Intelligence**: The ability to understand, appreciate, and produce music.
6. **Interpersonal Intelligence**: The ability to understand other people.
7. **Intrapersonal Intelligence**: The ability to understand oneself.
8. **Naturalist Intelligence**: The ability to be sensitive to and appreciative of the natural world.
9. **Existential Intelligence**: The ability to consider life's greater meaning.

Often lessons naturally address several of Gardner's intelligences. In the sample unit outlined earlier, students read about and discuss bullying (linguistic intelligence). They apply their findings to their own experience (intrapersonal intelligence), and they communicate with each other and with preservice teachers regarding bullying (interpersonal intelligence). With the understanding that no two students will have the same combination of intelligences as they approach their learning, it is wise to offer options that allow students to build their skills and knowledge based in a mode of thinking in which they feel comfortable. The expectations or end results (CCSS) are the same. Remember, Wiggins and McTighe likened BD to a road map. You want to have a destination in mind when you look at that map. The beauty of combining BD and CCSS is the flexibility that allows teachers and students to individualize the journey to those end results. By keeping well-respected theorists like Dewey, Bloom, and Gardner as our backseat drivers (in the best sense of the phrase!), we are sure to travel with our students on the path to knowledge that works best for them.

Part I

Reading

2 The Benefits of CCSS for the Teaching of Reading

We read deeply for varied reasons, most of them familiar: that we cannot know enough people profoundly enough that we need to know ourselves better; that we require knowledge, not just of self and others, but of the way things are. Yet the strongest, most authentic motive for deep reading of the now much abused traditional canon is the search for a difficult pleasure.

—Harold Bloom *(How to Read and Why)*

We chose to begin with Bloom's quote because it focuses on the pleasure that comes from mastering the task of reading. For many of our students, reading complex texts is difficult, but we hope that the rewards of unlocking the meaning of such texts are worth the struggle. How do we know that our students are having difficulty understanding complex texts? Of course, we can base such a statement on our own experiences or observation, but in addition, research supports this assertion. According to the results from ACT's *National Curriculum Survey* (2009a), both teachers and college instructors agreed that college readiness and workforce readiness require analogous knowledge and skills. However, only approximately two thirds of high school teachers reported that they believed that their students were ready for the demands of college reading. Students today are not prepared for college-level reading, and not even half could achieve the benchmark score in reading (ACT, 2006, 2009b). Compounding this unfortunate situation is that the majority of teachers lower their expectations for students they believe are not bound for college (ACT, 2010).

In this chapter, we will introduce the Common Core State Standards (CCSS) for Reading and provide commentary on the value of each of the Anchor Standards for increasing student college and career readiness. We hope that by teaching to these standards, teachers will be able to help students enjoy the "difficult pleasure," as described by Bloom, that results from reading well.

For easy reference, the Anchor Standards for Reading that we will reference throughout this chapter are listed below (see Table 2.1). Shaded citations within the chapter come directly from these Anchor Standards. At the end of the chapter, we will go beyond the more general Anchor Standards and examine the 6–8, 9–10, and 11–12 grade-specific standards for "Key Ideas and Details."

Table 2.1   Anchor Standards for Reading (National Governors Association Center for Best Practices [NGA]/Council of Chief State School Officers [CCSSO], 2010, p. 35)

READING

Key Ideas and Details

1. Read closely to determine what the text says explicitly and to make logical inferences from it; cite specific textual evidence when writing or speaking to support conclusions drawn from the text.

2. Determine central ideas or themes of a text and analyze their development; summarize the key supporting details and ideas.

3. Analyze in detail where, when, why, and how events, ideas, and characters develop and interact over the course of a text.

Craft and Structure

4. Interpret words and phrases as they are used in a text, including determining technical, connotative, and figurative meanings, and explain how specific word choices shape meaning or tone.

5. Analyze the structure of texts, including how specific sentences, paragraphs, and larger portions of the text (e.g., a section or chapter) relate to each other and the whole.

6. Assess how point of view or purpose shapes the content and style of a text.

Integration of Knowledge and Ideas

7. Synthesize and apply information presented in diverse ways (e.g., through words, images, graphs, and video) in print and digital sources in order to answer questions, solve problems, or compare modes of presentation.

8. Delineate and evaluate the reasoning and rhetoric within a text, including assessing whether the evidence provided is relevant and sufficient to support the text's claims.

9. Analyze how two or more texts address similar themes or topics in order to build knowledge or to compare the approaches the authors take.

Range and Level of Text Complexity

10. Read complex texts independently, proficiently, and fluently, sustaining concentration, monitoring comprehension, and, when useful, rereading.

KEY IDEAS AND DETAILS

ACT established a baseline against which to measure the effectiveness of the implementation of the CCSS by evaluating a quarter-million 11th-grade students in several states throughout the United States. They found that "only 31% of students are performing at a college- and career-ready level with respect to successfully understanding complex text" (ACT, 2010, p. 5). The "Key Ideas and Details" Anchor Standards for Reading address the need for the development of better skills for deciphering meaning of text ranging from a basic understanding to a more nuanced interpretation of meaning:

> 1. Read closely to determine what the text says explicitly and to make logical inferences from it; cite specific textual evidence when writing or speaking to support conclusions drawn from the text.
>
> 2. Determine central ideas or themes of a text and analyze their development; summarize the key supporting details and ideas.
>
> 3. Analyze how and why individuals, events, and ideas develop and interact over the course of a text.

This set of Anchor Standards supports reading development for 21st-century learners through the balance of the types of thinking skills that would fall in various sections of Bloom's Taxonomy from basic understanding ("determine what the text says explicitly") to higher order thinking ("make logical inferences," "analyze"). This balance addresses the need for change that Grant Wiggins (2010) demanded:

> Here is our problem in a nutshell. Students are taught formulas that they learn and spit back unthinkingly—regardless of subject matter—all in the name of "meeting standards." Yet, as so many assessment results reveal, a large portion of U.S. students are so literal minded that they are incapable of solving fairly simple questions requiring interpretation and transfer—which is surely the point of the state standards. (p. 51)

Therefore, in the name of meeting standards, students need to be taught on the basic level how to extract the main ideas of a text *and* also on a higher level how to engage in textual analysis and evaluation. The "Key Ideas and Details" Anchor Standards address these needs.

CRAFT AND STRUCTURE

ACT stated that we must "ensure that students gain sufficient understanding of how language varies by context; how to use language effectively for different audiences, purposes, and tasks; and how to gain and use a vocabulary adequate for college and careers" (2010, p. 5). The "Craft and Structure" Anchor Standards for Reading address awareness of language, construct, and style:

> 4. Interpret words and phrases as they are used in a text, including determining technical, connotative, and figurative meanings, and analyze how specific word choices shape meaning or tone.
>
> 5. Analyze the structure of texts including how specific sentences, paragraphs, and larger portions of the text (e.g., a section, chapter, scene, or stanza) relate to each other and the whole.
>
> 6. Assess how point of view or purpose shapes the content and style of a text.

According to ACT, fewer than half of students have the ability to acquire an expansive vocabulary and to use language at the college and career readiness level (ACT, 2010). This is particularly upsetting because with texting and e-mailing joining or perhaps overtaking face-to-face and phone conversation as common modes of communication, an understanding of the power of words has never been as important as it is today. More and more of our words are documented in print and on our cell phones and computers. The first Anchor Standard within "Craft and Structure" guides students to deeply consider the meaning of the words they read or write. With the guidance of this Anchor Standard, teachers and students focus not only on how words create a basic meaning, but on the subtle differences that word choice (connotation) or phrases (figurative language) can make.

It is important to note the clear connection between the development of analytical reading skills and students' development as writers and speakers. If students can assess the use of language in the works they are reading, then they can become critical of their own writing or speaking and be sure that they are expressing themselves in the manner in which they desire. This connection between reading comprehension and self-expression was examined by Michael Skube, a professor of journalism at Elon University. In a piece for *The Washington Post*, Skube (2006) connected his students' limited vocabulary with their lack of reading:

> In our better private universities and flagship state schools today, it's hard to find a student who graduated from high school with much lower than a 3.5 GPA, and not uncommon to find students whose GPA's were 4.0 or higher. They somehow got these suspect grades without having read much. Or if they did read, they've given it up. And it shows—in their writing and even in their conversation. (Skube, 2006, para. 4)

Skube offered an explanation for this paradox: "[K]ids don't read for pleasure. And because they don't read, they are less able to navigate the language.

If words are the coins of their thoughts, they're working with little more than pocket change" (2006, para. 18). If students become more skilled as readers, it stands to reason that they will develop better vocabulary and better judgment in regards to how to use that vocabulary.

The second "Craft and Structure" Anchor Standard continues to address the effective use of language by moving to a bigger picture—structure. Much like Skube's (2006) observations regarding vocabulary development, if students can make a connection between the recognition of structure within a work and the effect of that structure, they can apply their understanding to make better decisions when crafting their own writing.

The final "Craft and Structure" Anchor Standard calls for students to assess how point of view or purpose shapes the style or content of a text. An awareness of this within their reading can help students develop the voice that expresses their meaning in their own writing.

INTEGRATION OF KNOWLEDGE AND IDEAS

ACT connected the reading skills developed in English Language Arts (ELA) with the skills needed in other content areas. According to ACT (2010), schools must "ensure that teachers in these subject areas [other than ELA] use their unique content knowledge to foster students' ability to read, write, and communicate in the various disciplines" (p. 5). The Anchor Standards for "Integration of Knowledge and Ideas" within the Reading Strand address this need for improvement.

A key element of the CCSS for reading is developing the reading comprehension skills of students in various disciplines (e.g., social studies, science). This is essential as students lack the necessary skills to read and write to learn content (Kamil, 2003). As students ascend the grades and face increasingly complex literacy tasks in different subject areas, reading can become a difficult process. Teaching nonfiction texts is essential in enhancing students' success in the classroom. Explicitly teaching students how to read and understand discipline-specific texts will help students become more effective readers and learners of the subject matter; it will also prepare them for life.

Being able to apply the reading skills that we have taught students outside of the ELA is the first step to applying those skills to life outside of school. The "Integration of Knowledge and Ideas" Anchor Standards create guidelines for students to apply their skills outside of the ELA classroom:

7. Synthesize and apply information presented in diverse ways (e.g., through words, images, graphs, and video) in print and digital sources in order to answer questions, solve problems, or compare modes of presentation.

8. Delineate and evaluate the reasoning and rhetoric within a text, including assessing whether the evidence provided is relevant and sufficient to support the text's claims.

9. Analyze how two or more texts address similar themes or topics in order to build knowledge or to compare the approaches the authors take.

These Anchor Standards include verbs that align with the higher order thinking skills in Bloom's Taxonomy. Words such as *synthesize, apply, delineate, evaluate,* and *analyze* denote advanced and sophisticated cognitive processing of information. College- and career-ready students must be able to break down information (analyze), solve problems by using facts and knowledge in different ways (apply), integrate knowledge and ideas (synthesize), and assess the validity of and make judgments on ideas and works (evaluate).

If purposeful education is the preparation for college and career through the development of skills that students will use once they are in those settings (and as Dewey advocated), it is logical to practice the application of skills across disciplines. Sometimes application happens naturally. We have all enjoyed the light bulb moment when a student says, "This is like what I am studying in _____." However, all too often in our schools, subjects are taught in their own wing or on their own floor (e.g., math classes held on the third floor and ELA on the second floor). This is unfortunately reflective of our approach to educating our students. The types of thinking used in math are not limited to math. The types of thinking utilized in ELA are not limited to ELA, but students and teachers alike need the CCSS to help guide them toward better integration. After all, when students enter their careers, it is not likely that they will be asked to focus only on math for 40 minutes and then on ELA for 40 minutes. Rather, they will need to utilize a variety of thinking skills across a variety of disciplines.

Students can more easily see the *content*-based connections among their classes. The challenge is getting students to realize that the reading *skills* they use in ELA can be transferred to other subject area work. We must be cognizant of encouraging students to make connections in relation to the thinking skills they are using when they read for any of their courses. This is especially important as students are applying their skills to several mediums through which we gather information (screen images, video, quantitative data). If students can recognize the need to transfer their skills across subject areas, it follows that they can see how the same skills can be applied to the various mediums of expression that they are encountering.

The second and third "Integration of Knowledge and Ideas" Anchor Standards call for students to be critical of the pieces that they read. They must consider the validity of their sources. Also, once they decide on more than one piece as strong sources of information, they should be able to compare how two or more writers approach a similar topic or theme. This incorporates analysis of style and bias, higher order tasks that are challenging for students. Add complex texts to the mix, and students are often unable to comprehend content. The majority of professors and nearly half of employers, according to a study by Achieve (2007), find that students' inability to read complex texts is a serious problem. The descriptors for "Integration of Knowledge and Ideas" provide guidelines by which teachers can create purposeful learning that helps students address their need for improvement.

RANGE OF READING
LEVEL AND COMPLEXITY

Not only do students need to develop more advanced thinking skills, they need to be able to apply those skills to more sophisticated texts. There is a discrepancy between the difficulty of high school texts versus that of college-level texts (NGA Center/CCSSO, 2010c). College textbooks are more challenging as are nonfiction texts that college instructors typically assign. On average, workplace reading is more advanced than high school reading. College professors expect students to read independently and with no support as soon as they enter their classrooms, as opposed to high school teachers who provide scaffolding for students and guide them through their reading (NGA Center/CCSSO, 2010c). Based on the finding that only 31% of students are able to understand complex texts, ACT (2010) stated, "To help prepare all students for the challenges of reading at the college and career readiness level, states should ensure that students are reading progressively more complex texts as they advance through the grades" (p. 5).

Students need to be able to independently apply higher order thinking skills to increasingly complex texts as they progress through their education. The "Range of Reading and Level of Text Complexity" Anchor Standard reflects this need:

> 10. Read and comprehend complex literary and informational texts independently and proficiently.

Students need to read a range of sophisticated texts, which include classic American literature, poetry, and Shakespearean texts as well as informational texts. Students need to practice a range of thinking, from making connections to evaluating the verity and quality of writing in various sources. In measuring the complexity of texts, the CCSS consider three factors:

1. Qualitative evaluation of the text: Levels of meaning, structure, language conventionality and clarity, and knowledge demands

2. Quantitative evaluation of the text: Readability measures and other scores of text complexity

3. Matching reader to text and task: Reader variables (such as motivation, knowledge, and experiences) and task variables (such as purpose and the complexity generated by the task assigned and the questions posed)

(NGA Center/CCSSO, 2010c)

Appendix A of the CCSS Document for ELA includes an extensive explanation of the measures for the three factors listed previously. To give you a general idea of their meaning, we are including a few samples for each factor. Within the qualitative factor, levels of meaning may range from explicit purpose to implicit. Structure may range from chronologic to nonchronologic (i.e., using flashback or thematic organization). Language may be literal or figurative, contemporary or archaic. Knowledge demands may include a perspective that is similar to the reader's or one that is very different, many allusions to other texts or very few, general vocabulary/content base or very specific content understanding (NGA Center/CCSSO, 2010c).

The quantitative factor for reading includes the measurement of word length, sentence length, frequency of familiar versus unfamiliar vocabulary, syntactic complexity, and cohesiveness of text. If you are reading this and feeling overwhelmed, you are not alone. In a discussion of the Quantitative factor for "Range, Quality, and Complexity of Student Reading," the CCSS compared various tests. One that stood out as a strong measure was the nonprofit service Coh-Metrix. Though this seems to be a more efficient and reliable system than its competitors, it is still not flawless. The CCSS stated that the "greatest value of these factors may well be the promise they offer of more advanced and usable tools yet to come" (NGA Center/CCSSO, 2010c, p. 7).

Given the complexity of the quantitative factor, it is heartening to see the CCSS include a human factor by matching reader to text and task by considering what the reader brings to the reading—cognitive capabilities, motivation, knowledge, and background knowledge (Rand Reading Study Group, 2002). Our students change from year to year. Their strengths and needs change from year to year. They have different ways of learning and processing information, as Gardner would argue. Measuring and understanding our students is daunting enough. The CCSS hope to help with the measuring and understanding of the literature that meets our students' needs by providing us with the guideline of the three factors (qualitative evaluation of text, quantitative evaluation of text, and matching reader to text and task).

The CCSS (2010c) provide examples of the analysis of text complexity in Appendix A. They include a sample evaluation of *Narrative of the Life of Frederick Douglass* (see http://www.corestandards.org/assets/Appendix_A.pdf, p. 12).

Not only do the CCSS provide a frame for evaluating reading choices for students, they provide an extensive book list for ELA, History/Social Studies, Science, and Technical Subjects for each grade level. The CCSS stress that these are "guideposts" or "exemplars," not dictated curriculum. Titles include *Little Women* by Louisa May Alcott (1869); *The Adventures of Tom Sawyer* by Mark Twain (1876); "The Road Not Taken" by Robert Frost (1915); "Letter on Thomas Jefferson" by John Adams (1776); and *Narrative of the Life of Frederick Douglass, an American Slave* by Frederick Douglass (1845) (NGA Center/CCSSO, 2010c, p. 58). To further assist teachers in making informed decisions regarding appropriate texts for their students, the CCSS (2010d) list text exemplars in Appendix B (see http://www.corestandards.org/assets/Appendix_B.pdf).

The importance of evaluating "Range, Quality, and Complexity of Student Reading" is emphasized in the introduction to Appendix A. The CCSS note what distinguished the high-performing students from lower performing students on the ACT preliminary test was not the ability to make inferences, determine the main idea, or define vocabulary in context. Rather, it was the ability of high-performing students to work with complex texts that set them apart from their peers. Teaching that emphasized only "'higher-order' or 'critical' thinking was insufficient to ensure that students were ready for college and careers: what students could read, in terms of its complexity, was at least as important as what they could do with what they read" (NGA Center/CCSSO, 2010c, p. 2).

It is important for teachers to help students enhance their reading and analytical skills; however, as the findings above show, it is not enough to teach students how to comprehend "Key Ideas and Details," analyze "Craft and Structure," and apply "Integration of Knowledge and Ideas"; we must help them to develop these skills with an increased "Range of Reading and Level of Text Complexity."

A CLOSER LOOK

Let's look at the grade-specific standards for the first set of standards under "Key Ideas and Details" for Literature 6–8 and 9–12 and for Informational Texts 6–8 and 9–12 to determine what students need to be able to know and do by the end of each grade band (see Tables 2.2–2.5). Within the 6–8 grade-specific standards for Literature and for Informational Text, students need to provide textual support for their analysis of text. Students in Grades 9–10 need to provide strong and thorough evidence, and in Grades 11–12 they must "determine where the text leaves matters uncertain." In other words, by the end of high school, students must be able to not only extract and analyze the main ideas of a work of literature but also evaluate the clarity of the text.

The same advanced thinking is required with regard to the second set of grade-specific standards for "Key Ideas and Details." In Grades 6–12, students need to be able to determine the central idea of a text and provide an objective summary of the text. The difference that distinguishes the grade levels (6–8, 9–10, and 11–12) is that in the lower grades, students need to analyze one theme and how it is shaped by textual details, whereas in the higher grades, they must analyze two or more themes and how they produce a complex account.

To illustrate knowledge and skill progression as students advance in grade level, let's consider another example from "Integration of Knowledge and Ideas for Literature." The grade-specific standards state that students in Grades 6 and 7 compare and contrast the experience of text in different mediums but in Grade 7 also analyze the effects of techniques on each medium. In Grade 8, students analyze and evaluate the relationship between a live or filmed production of a story or drama and the text or script. In Grades 9–10, students analyze the subject or key scene in two different artistic mediums, and in Grades 11–12, they analyze multiple interpretations of literary texts (e.g., recorded or live production of a play or recorded novel or poetry) and evaluate each one. In the higher grades, students must make meaning of multiple literary texts of increasing complexity; in addition, the CCSS recommend that one work be a play by Shakespeare and another play by an American dramatist. The examples given for interpretations of literature (namely, *recorded or live production of a play, recorded novel or poetry*) illustrate how multimodal learning—an important piece of the CCSS—is infused into the standards.

Table 2.2 Reading Standards for Literature 6–8 (NGA/CCSSO, 2010b, p. 36)

Grade 6 Students	Grade 7 Students	Grade 8 Students
Key Ideas and Details	*Key Ideas and Details*	*Key Ideas and Details*
1. Cite textual evidence to support analysis of what the text says explicitly as well as inferences drawn from the text.	1. Cite several pieces of textual evidence to support analysis of what the text says explicitly as well as inferences drawn from the text.	1. Cite the textual evidence that most strongly supports an analysis of what the text says explicitly as well as inferences drawn from the text.
2. Determine a theme or central idea of a text and how it is conveyed through particular details; provide a summary of the text distinct from personal opinions or judgments.	2. Determine a theme or central idea of a text and analyze its development over the course of the text; provide an objective summary of the text.	2. Determine a theme or central idea of a text and analyze its development over the course of the text, including its relationship to the characters, setting, and plot; provide an objective summary of the text.
3. Describe how a particular story's or drama's plot unfolds in a series of episodes as well as how the characters respond or change as the plot moves toward a resolution.	3. Analyze how particular elements of a story or drama interact (e.g., how setting shapes the characters or plot).	3. Analyze how particular lines of dialogue or incidents in a story or drama propel the action, reveal aspects of a character, or provoke a decision.

Table 2.3 Reading Standards for Informational Text 6–8 (NGA/CCSSO, 2010b, p. 39)

Grade 6 Students	Grade 7 Students	Grade 8 Students
Key Ideas and Details	*Key Ideas and Details*	*Key Ideas and Details*
1. Cite textual evidence to support analysis of what the text says explicitly as well as inferences drawn from the text.	1. Cite several pieces of textual evidence to support analysis of what the text says explicitly as well as inferences drawn from the text.	1. Cite textual evidence that most strongly supports an analysis of what the text says explicitly as well as inferences drawn from the text.
2. Determine a central idea of a text and how it is conveyed through particular details; provide a summary of the text distinct from personal opinions or judgments.	2. Determine two or more central ideas in a text and analyze their development over the course of the text; provide an objective summary of the text.	2. Determine a central idea of a text and analyze its development over the course of the text, including its relationship to supporting ideas; provide an objective summary of the text.

(Continued)

| Table 2.3 | (Continued) |

Grade 6 Students	Grade 7 Students	Grade 8 Students
Key Ideas and Details	*Key Ideas and Details*	*Key Ideas and Details*
3. Analyze in detail how a key individual, event, or idea is introduced, illustrated, and elaborated in a text (e.g., through examples or anecdotes).	3. Analyze the interactions between individuals, events, and ideas in a text (e.g., how ideas influence individuals or events, or how individuals influence ideas or events).	3. Analyze how a text makes connections among and distinctions between individuals, ideas, or events (e.g., through comparisons, analogies, or categories).

| Table 2.4 | Reading Standards for Literature 9–12 (NGA/CCSSO, 2010b, p. 38) |

Grades 9–10 Students	Grades 11–12 Students
Key Ideas and Details	*Key Ideas and Details*
1. Cite strong and thorough textual evidence to support analysis of what the text says explicitly as well as inferences drawn from the text.	1. Cite strong and thorough textual evidence to support analysis of what the text says explicitly as well as inferences drawn from the text, including determining where the text leaves matters uncertain.
2. Determine a theme or central idea of a text and analyze in detail its development over the course of the text, including how it emerges and is shaped and refined by specific details; provide an objective summary of the text.	2. Determine two or more themes or central ideas of a text and analyze their development over the course of the text, including how they interact and build on one another to produce a complex account; provide an objective summary of the text.

| Table 2.5 | Reading Standards for Informational Text 9–12 (NGA/CCSSO, 2010b, p. 40) |

Grades 9–10 Students	Grades 11–12 Students
Key Ideas and Details	*Key Ideas and Details*
1. Cite strong and thorough textual evidence to support analysis of what the text says explicitly as well as inferences drawn from the text.	1. Cite strong and thorough textual evidence to support analysis of what the text says explicitly as well as inferences drawn from the text, including determining where the text leaves matters uncertain.

Grades 9–10 Students	Grades 11–12 Students
Key Ideas and Details	*Key Ideas and Details*
2. Determine a central idea of a text and analyze its development over the course of the text, including how it emerges and is shaped and refined by specific details; provide an objective summary of the text.	2. Determine two or more central ideas of a text and analyze their development over the course of the text, including how they interact and build on one another to provide a complex analysis; provide an objective summary of the text.

CONCLUSION

As you read this chapter and take in the standards, we hope that you are thinking to yourself, "I do this already!" If so, then the CCSS should serve as reinforcement of the good decisions that you are making regarding your instruction. Perhaps you have thought to yourself, "I would like to help my students be more aware of _____." If so, then the standards are helping to make you more aware of a need for enhanced instruction.

Bloom's quote at the start of this chapter reminds us that reading is a difficult task, but one that yields great pleasure for those who do it well. Pleasure is not simply happiness in this case. Pleasure is the self-satisfaction that comes with greater understanding of a concept and better understanding of effective means of expression. In the next chapter, we present reading lessons that include the CCSS for Reading. We hope that they will serve as models for your own lesson planning and guide you in helping your students experience the "difficult pleasure" that is reading.

We have all felt that a reading lesson or unit is going along beautifully and then had that eye-opening moment when we realized that perhaps it was not going as well as we thought. When Maureen was teaching *Romeo and Juliet*, she thought that her students fully comprehended the balcony scene and that they were appreciative of the metaphors and the tone set forth by the characters. It was time for a treat, so they watched Franco Zeffirelli's movie version of the scene. After seeing Juliet with her long, dark hair atop her balcony, Mallory, a sweet ninth-grade girl, asked: "When is he going to climb up her hair?" Ugh! What went wrong? Did Mallory comprehend the passage when presented in text form? Was it just the visual (the long hair) that caused the confusion? What could Maureen have done as her teacher to ensure her comprehension? The CCSS for Reading might have helped Maureen better assess Mallory's comprehension and ability to analyze the scene. Do you have students like Mallory? If so, how do you help them succeed in reading? How do you help them recognize their perceived "completion" of a writing piece as a place to start revising? How can the CCSS help?

QUESTIONS/CHALLENGES/ PONDERING POINTS

1. How has the 21st century changed your perspective on teaching reading?

2. How complex are the texts that you are assigning to your students?

3. In what ways do your students need to improve their reading skills?

4. How do you design curriculum that addresses your students' needs for improvement?

5. How do you modify instruction to promote the development of students' reading skills?

Reading Lessons From the Classroom 3

INTRODUCTION

In this chapter, we will present three lessons that we believe are particularly effective for addressing the Common Core State Standards (CCSS) for Reading. In the first lesson for Grades 6–8, students discuss and analyze two texts, *Journey of the Sparrows* and *The Arrival*, and retell the story of the former using a graphic novel format. The second lesson, based on *Macbeth*, is appropriate for Grades 9–10 and requires students to analyze one of *Macbeth*'s soliloquies and use its structure to compose their own soliloquies. Lastly, the Grades 11–12 lesson on Lincoln's Gettysburg Address engages students in a critical examination of well-known presidential speeches.

Within the first lesson, students examine how the authors of two very different texts (*Journey of the Sparrows* is a young adult novel, and *The Arrival* is a graphic novel) convey the experience of immigrating to the United States. They use their summarizing skills and their understanding of the effectiveness of some of the elements of a graphic novel to create a comic book version of an assigned chapter of *Journey of the Sparrows*. Students engaged in the lesson on *Macbeth* analyze a soliloquy meant to explain/inform the viewers of Macbeth's vision of a dagger and his feelings of temptation. Then they write their own soliloquies based on the Bard's work. In contrast to the works of fiction discussed in the first two lessons, the third lesson involves informational text. Students examine the content and style of Lincoln's Gettysburg Address and consider how he and other presidents who have followed him may influence contemporary political speakers. In all three lessons, evaluation of the core text is central. Students must cite specific sections of text as evidence to support their analysis.

As you read through these lessons and as you develop your own lessons, we encourage you to focus on how you can guide your students to meet the CCSS for Reading that you examined in Chapter 2. Two sets of questions for reflection are listed below—specific questions pertaining to Reading Anchor Standards and general questions regarding Lesson Design.

READING ANCHOR STANDARDS REFLECTIVE QUESTIONS

How does the lesson require students to do one or more of the following?

1. Determine what the text says explicitly and make logical inferences from it?

2. Cite specific textual evidence when writing or speaking to support conclusions drawn from the text?

3. Determine the main ideas and details of a text?

4. Analyze the development of ideas in a text?

5. Interpret words or phrases in a text and analyze how they shape meaning?

6. Analyze the structure of a text and analyze how sentences, paragraphs, and larger portions of the text shape meaning?

7. Assess how point of view of a text shapes the meaning and style of a text?

8. Integrate and evaluate the content of the text presented in diverse media and formats?

9. Evaluate the argument and claims in a text?

10. Analyze how two or more texts address similar themes or topics?

LESSON DESIGN REFLECTIVE QUESTIONS

1. How does the lesson require close and multiple readings of grade-level complex text (classic, contemporary, or informational)?

2. How does my questioning require students to use the text as support for their interpretations/arguments?

3. How does the lesson incorporate varied thinking skills (e.g., read, summarize, analyze, interpret)? (Bloom)

4. How does the lesson include the three components of Backward Design: (a) desired results, (b) acceptable evidence, and (c) learning experiences?

5. How do I differentiate instruction, materials, and expectations for this particular lesson so that struggling students can be successful?

6. How does the lesson provide opportunities for technology/media use?

7. How does the lesson include research-based instructional strategies to promote effective teaching?

8. How can the lesson present opportunities for interdisciplinary connections?

9. How does the lesson provide opportunities for students with varied Multiple Intelligences to be successful? (Gardner)

10. How do I present the lesson in a way that encourages students to see the value of what they are learning (e.g., service learning, college- and career-readiness skills)? (Dewey)

Lesson Plan Template

TOPIC:

Journey of the Sparrows Graphic Novel Retelling (Grades 6–8)

CCSS STRAND:

Reading

TEXT TYPES AND PURPOSES:

Convey Experience

TIMING:

5 class periods

BACKWARD DESIGN COMPONENTS:

DESIRED RESULTS/CCSS ADDRESSED:

- Read closely to determine explicit and inferential meaning from *The Arrival* and *Journey of the Sparrows*. Use evidence to support this meaning [R.1].

- Analyze how and why individuals, events, and ideas develop and interact over the course of the two novels [R.3].

- Summarize the main ideas and details of a particular chapter [R.2, R.3].

- Analyze how the two novels address the theme of immigration and compare the approaches the authors take [R.9].

ACCEPTABLE EVIDENCE:

- Interpretation of *The Arrival* handout

- Chapter slides (rough draft and final draft)

LEARNING EXPERIENCES AND INSTRUCTION:

- Day 1—Analyze *The Arrival* and make connections to *Journey of the Sparrows*.

- Days 2–3—Create chapter slides

- Day 4—Peer-response to chapter slides.

- Day 5—Revise chapter slides and celebrate work.

STRATEGIES:

- Guidance and Monitoring

- Discussion

- Cooperative Learning

- Writing Process

- Modeling

SUPPLEMENTAL RESOURCES:

- Students read articles about immigration (local immigration issues and news).

TECHNOLOGY/MEDIA OPPORTUNITIES:

- Students represent the novel through multimodalities using Microsoft Photo Story.

SERVICE LEARNING LINK:

- Students in other classes complete the same lesson for other texts. To review for final exams, they visit each other's classrooms and read each class's chapter slides.

- Students write letters to immigrants in their community inquiring about life in their native country and their experiences migrating to the United States. Based on these letters, students inform local stores about foods that local immigrants have difficulty finding and/or they create visual representations of the immigrant stories gathered to display at local businesses.

VARIATIONS:

- Use with other texts with immigration themes, such as *Lupita Manana* by Patricia Beaty; *Barrio Boy* by Ernesto Galarza; *Kids Like Me: Voices of the Immigrant Experience* by Judith M. Blohm and Terri Lapinsky; *My Name Is Yoon* by Helen Recorvits and Gabi Swiatkowska.

- During the gallery walk students write a response on each slide and respond to other classmates' comments.

- Students make text-to-text connections by selecting a picture from *The Arrival* to illustrate an experience in *Journey of the Sparrows*.

JOURNEY OF THE SPARROWS
GRAPHIC NOVEL RETELLING

(Grades 6–8; Convey Experience)

Vicky and Maureen Speak

Literature with immigration themes is an excellent vehicle to teach all students about the hardships of migrating to a new country, suffering prejudicial injustices, and maintaining hope for a better life. This type of literature appeals not only to diverse students who can relate to the characters and situations in the stories but also to middle school students, in general, who are dealing with issues of growing up, transitioning into adolescence, and developing their personal identities. *Journey of the Sparrows* (2002) by Fran Leeper Buss is just one example of literature with immigration themes that works well with all middle school students. It is about the arduous and terrifying journey of a Salvadorian teenager, María, and her siblings across the U.S. border and then north into Chicago and the hard life they endure in their new country, always fearing deportation.

When teaching this novel, we want students to be able to do three things: (a) develop cross-cultural understanding and empathy toward people who are different from them; (b) understand how the themes of the novel are conveyed through the use of figurative language, specifically metaphor; (c) be able to recognize character development over the course of the text [R.3].

We do this in a creative way by using the graphic novel, *The Arrival*, as a model for telling a story through pictures. Without words, plot, theme, character development, and mood are conveyed. The transcendence of these elements beyond print emphasizes their power. In this visual age, students may find it easier or more appealing to interpret pictures rather than print.

 THEORY LINK (Dewey): Developing citizenry—students are enhancing their understanding of diversity.

Materials Needed

Paper and pens

PowerPoint technology

Handouts

Timing

5 class periods

Day 1—Analyze *The Arrival* and make connections to *Journey of the Sparrows.*

Days 2–3—Create chapter slides.

Day 4—Peer-response to chapter slides

Day 5—Revise chapter slides and celebrate work.

Day 1

After completing the novel, the teacher shares a video clip without any sound. We recommend using a popular movie with which students may be familiar. Students view the soundless clip without any explanation. After a minute, the teacher asks students what was happening in the clip. In spite of the lack of sound, most students will be able to discuss some plot development, mood, and characterization. When the teacher asks students how they were able to recognize these elements, they discuss how they inferred this information from visual cues. This activity prepares students for viewing and interpreting the graphic novel *The Arrival*, by Shaun Tan [R.1], which is a wordless book that depicts the experiences of the main character migrating to the United States. The reader relies on images, including symbols (e.g., the strange creature), to create meaning from the story.

Students can work together as a class to interpret this novel and infer meaning. Just as in reading print, students must provide evidence to support their interpretation of this work (**Handout 1**) [R.1]. Depending on the level at which the teacher chooses to analyze the book, this activity may take multiple class periods.

After reading *The Arrival*, students can compare the experiences of the main characters in the graphic novel with the experiences of the main characters in *Journey of the Sparrows* [R.9]. This comparison of print and image opens up a discussion regarding how authors and artists convey their meaning through their medium. This is a great place to use a Venn diagram. Students can consider common elements such as vibrant color versus black and white, literal versus figurative, and structure (chronological order vs. flashback, thematic order, compare/contrast). They can discuss the impact that images have as compared with print (most students will comment on the immediacy of images). Some students may comment on the value of narration and dialogue in print for making meaning more explicit.

Days 2–3

Students work in groups to create a graphic novel version of *Journey of the Sparrows*. Each group is assigned a different chapter. For each chapter, students must develop four PowerPoint slides with images and print (**Handout 2**). By limiting the end product to four slides, students must reflect and consider the most pertinent main ideas and details of the chapter [R.2, R.3].

The teacher monitors the group work. When finished, students print out their slides and submit them to the teacher who posts them on the wall. Groups exchange graphic chapters and complete a peer-response handout. The class discusses ways to improve the graphic novel version and make it fluent and coherent.

DIFFERENTIATION TIP: We recommend heterogeneous grouping. Students (or the teacher) may assign roles within the groups based on talents and skills.

TECH CONNECTION: The slides in PowerPoint parallel the boxes in the graphic novel.

THEORY LINK (Gardner): Appeals to Visual-Spatial Intelligence.

THEORY LINK (Bloom): Students *interpret* and *analyze* the novel and *synthesize* the content visually.

THEORY LINK (Gardner): Appeals to Interpersonal Intelligence.

THEORY LINK (Bloom): Students *evaluate* each other's work.

Day 4

Groups revise their graphic chapters in class using the feedback during the peer-response stage the day before. They print the revised slides at home and bring them to class the following day.

Day 5

The teacher collects the revised printed slides and posts them on the wall. Students do a gallery walk and read the graphic novel version from beginning to end. The class can discuss how the novel compares with the visual representation; which medium they prefer and why; what additional slides they think could come before the beginning or after the ending that would still stay true to the essence of the story.

In this lesson, students are engaged in complex activities. They are reading and analyzing literary texts (traditional and wordless), making text-to-text connections (soundless movie, *The Arrival, Journey of the Sparrows*), creating new texts (chapter slides) using multimedia, and evaluating their peers' work. They experience reading text through not only traditional print but also a multitude of texts generated through visual art and technology.

HANDOUT 1

INTERPRETATION OF *THE ARRIVAL*

1. I believe that at this point in the book . . .
   (what is happening?)

2. Two images that support my belief are . . .

   a.

   b.

HANDOUT 2

JOURNEY OF THE SPARROWS— GRAPHIC NOVEL CHAPTER SLIDES

Overview

We will work together as a class to assemble completed PowerPoint visual representations of all of the chapters of *Journey of the Sparrows* into our own graphic novel.

Class Responsibilities

As a class we will agree upon several images of each character (with varied expressions) that will be available in a shared data folder. You can cut and paste these images into your PowerPoint slides.

Group Responsibilities

Creating

For this assignment, your group will be responsible for representing one chapter of *Journey of the Sparrows* in FOUR PowerPoint slides.

Your slides must include:

1. A clear representation of any important events (plot)

2. An accurate representation of the characters (characterization)

3. Any conflicts (person vs. self, person vs. person, person vs. society)

4. At least ONE symbol

5. A consideration of color as it connects with mood

6. At least TWO quotes from the narration, which include figurative language

7. At least TWO lines of dialogue—in voice bubbles

HANDOUT 3

PEER RESPONSE

You will be responsible for responding to the slides of your peers. Take the following into consideration:

1. Are the events clearly represented? Yes _____ No _____

   Give one example from a slide:

2. Are the characters clearly represented? Yes _____ No _____

   Give one example from a slide:

3. Do the slides include conflict (person vs. self, person vs. person, person vs. society)?
   Yes _____ No _____

   Give one example from a slide:

4. Do the slides include at least one symbol? Yes _____ No _____

   Give one example from a slide:

5. Do the slides connect color and mood? Yes _____ No _____

   Give one example from a slide:

6. Respond to one of the quotes from the narration that includes figurative language.

   (How do you feel? What do you think? What questions come to mind?)

7. Respond to one of the lines of dialogue—in voice bubbles.

   (How do you feel? What do you think? What questions come to mind?)

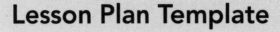

Lesson Plan Template

TOPIC:
Macbeth Soliloquy (Grades 9–10)

CCSS STRAND:
Reading

TEXTS TYPES AND PURPOSES:
Explain/Inform

TIMING:
3 class periods

BACKWARD DESIGN COMPONENTS:

DESIRED RESULTS/CCSS ADDRESSED:

- Understand the meaning of the passage [R.1, R.2, R.3, R.10].
- Analyze the use of sensory and figurative language [R.4, L.3].
- Explain how the theme applies to themselves by participating in the writing process in order to create their own soliloquies [W.2, W.5, W.6].

ACCEPTABLE EVIDENCE:

- Annotations on *Macbeth* soliloquy Handout 1
- Students' own soliloquies based on Shakespeare's theme and style

LEARNING EXPERIENCES AND INSTRUCTION:

- Day 1—Pre-read journal on temptation followed by reading and interpreting the soliloquy.
- Day 2—Draft temptation soliloquies based on Shakespeare's style.
- Day 3—Share, peer-response, revise, publish.

STRATEGIES:

- Guidance and Monitoring
- Cooperative Learning
- Writing Process
- Modeling

SUPPLEMENTAL RESOURCES:

Simplified text (see www .nosweatshakespeare.com/quotes/ soliloquies/macbeth-dagger-before-me.htm and www.bardweb.net/content/readings/ macbeth/lines.html).

TECHNOLOGY/MEDIA OPPORTUNITIES:

- View or listen to several versions of the soliloquy and discuss how differences in filming or acting influence meaning. Examples: Roman Polanski's version versus Patrick Stewart's stage version (consider lighting, tone of voice, pace of speaking, costuming).

SERVICE LEARNING LINK:

- Students write soliloquies specifically focused on what keeps them from doing their homework.
- Students share those soliloquies with younger students and help the younger students write their own soliloquies on the same topic.
- Students develop time-management strategies with younger students to help them avoid their temptations at homework time!

VARIATIONS:

- Use with other Shakespearean soliloquies or poems. Examples: Juliet's speech before drinking the potion in *Romeo and Juliet* (Theme: fear), "A Dream Deferred" by Langston Hughes (Theme: dreams that do not come to be).
- Use with speeches by other authors. Examples: "I'm Waiting" speech by Mama in *A Raisin in the Sun*, the coach's speech in *Miracle*.
- Use with popular song lyrics. Example: Taylor Swift songs tend to be popular with many students (and full of literary devices).
- Use as a reading-based activity with Reader/Writer Workshop model.

MACBETH SOLILOQUY

(Grades 9–10; Explain/Inform)

Maureen Speaks

Whenever I begin teaching a play by the Bard, inevitably, there are students who announce, "I don't get Shakespeare." The playwright's language is dense and intricate—a paradox for most high school students. My grandmother was an English teacher, and one of the best pieces of advice she gave me was to remember that with difficult texts, students do not need to understand every word. They need to be able to appreciate the best parts. The following activity helps students to do just that.

Materials Needed

Copy of Macbeth's dagger soliloquy

Paper and pens

Handouts

Timing

3 class periods

Day 1—Pre-read journal on temptation followed by reading and interpreting the soliloquy.

Day 2—Draft temptation soliloquies based on Shakespeare's style.

Day 3—Share, peer-response, revise, publish.

One of the most famous soliloquies in *Macbeth* is in Act II, Scene 1. Macbeth begins, "Is that a dagger which I see before me?" This is an important passage because it represents a pivotal moment in the play, the moment when Macbeth decides to kill Duncan. Though the witches and his wife have certainly influenced him prior to this, my students and I discuss how this is the last moment that he can choose to take another path. It is interesting to note that when he makes this evil choice to kill Duncan, he does so based on an apparition. This says something about Macbeth's character. He is so blinded by ambition that he is not thinking rationally. Shakespeare's use of sensory and figurative language to develop character and to address the theme of temptation makes this an excellent passage to use with students. By the end of the 3 days that we spend working with this soliloquy, I want students to be able to understand the meaning of the passage, analyze the use of sensory and figurative language, and explain how the theme applies to them by writing their own soliloquies.

Day 1

Before we read Macbeth's soliloquy, I ask students to write in their journals about temptation.

THEORY LINK (Bloom): Students exhibit *comprehension* of temptation and *application* to self.

THEORY LINK (Gardner): Appeals to Intrapersonal Intelligence.

DIFFERENTIATION TIP: There are many simplified Shakespearean texts available online.
Remember, ultimately, students need to be able to work with complex texts. Consider: What are you doing to enhance skills development?

THEORY LINK (Gardner): Appeals to Verbal-Linguistic Intelligence.

THEORY LINK (Bloom): Students are required to do more than *comprehend* basic meaning. They must *analyze* style.

I give them the following prompts: "What tempts you? What do you do when you are tempted? Do you try to resist? How does this make you feel?" [W.2]

If students are struggling to answer, I model a response for them—most likely involving cupcakes (my weakness) while a picture of a cupcake is displayed via PowerPoint for inspiration.

After focusing on our own experiences with temptation, we are ready to read what Macbeth has to say on the topic (**Handout 1**). First, students read the soliloquy on their own to try to understand the basic meaning [R.1, R.2, R.3, R.10]. They circle words that stand out and seem important, underline lines that appeal to them, annotate literary devices, and write question marks next to any lines that are unclear. Many lines are unclear! If needed, I provide students who are struggling with a simplified version of the text that they use alongside their reading of the original.

This parallel original/simplified textual reading enables students at different levels to comprehend the text. Next, we work together, taking the soliloquy line-by-line, phrase-by-phrase, word-by-word—whatever is needed until it all makes sense.

This usually involves my making a fool of myself, acting it out as we read. Once students have a basic understanding of the text, we conduct a more analytical reading for style rather than comprehension [R.4, L.3].

We consider literary elements, appeals to the senses, and strong diction. Not only do we work to recognize Shakespeare's stylistic choices, we discuss the effect of these choices. Does the temptation of the dagger alleviate some of Macbeth's guilt? How does the bloodiness add to the mood of the play? How does the personification of the stones ("stones prate of my whereabout") add to your understanding of Macbeth's paranoia? This type of analysis is key in helping students write about literature [R.4, L.3].

Day 2

Rather than writing an essay about Shakespeare's writing style (reading these would be very repetitive for me since we conducted the analysis together), students show their appreciation for Shakespeare's work by writing their own

"Is that a _____ I see before me?" speeches [W.2]. These speeches include key lines from the original that students find important and effective. They also include at least two original examples of figurative language. At first, this task seems daunting, but again, I model this for them using the temptation of cupcakes (**Handout 2**) and quickly they realize how anything that tempts us calls to most of our senses and inspires poetic language. Some of the most interesting student versions of this famous speech focus on food, the computer, Xbox, and most recently a poignant piece about the temptation of a girlfriend. Students get very invested in their work and are usually not only willing but eager to share it.

Day 3

Students pair up and exchange their soliloquies. The reader must circle the figurative language utilized by the writer [R.4, L.3]. This opportunity to practice literary analysis and to discuss findings is important, but, moreover, the support that students give to one another is inspiring. The readers often call me over to check out how great their friends' speeches are. I sit with each pair and give students feedback on their speeches. They also help each other with minor editing or revisions [W.5]. After the sharing process, students revise their work, taking into consideration all the constructive feedback that they received from their peers and from myself. I can happily report that this support and excitement actually makes it acceptable for students to read their soliloquies aloud to the class or to type up their soliloquies and publish them on the bulletin board in my room and on my webpage [W.6].

The result of this process is that all students, even the struggling readers, change from feeling trepidation about Shakespeare to feeling connected to this inaccessible-to-many author. In order to write like him, they must first understand him and appreciate his style. This lesson allows for a true blend of higher order thinking skills (analysis, evaluation, synthesis) and creative self-expression.

 THEORY LINK (Gardner): Appeals to Interpersonal Intelligence.

 THEORY LINK (Dewey): Purposeful learning—students are not just earning a grade. Their work is being published for their friends and family to view.

 TECH CONNECTION: Students could also post this on a blog or on their Facebook accounts.

 DIFFERENTIATION TIP: Students may also opt to record their soliloquies as podcasts.

HANDOUT 1

MACBETH—ACT II, SCENE 1

Directions: Complete the steps listed below:

1. Read the following soliloquy, and consider the basic meaning of the text.

2. Circle any words that stand out to you.

3. Underline any lines that appeal to the senses.

4. Label literary devices in the margins.

5. Write a question mark next to any phrases that do not make sense to you.

MACBETH

Is this a dagger which I see before me,

The handle toward my hand? Come, let me clutch thee.

I have thee not, and yet I see thee still.

Art thou not, fatal vision, sensible

To feeling as to sight? or art thou but

A dagger of the mind, a false creation,

Proceeding from the heat-oppressed brain?

I see thee yet, in form as palpable

As this which now I draw.

Thou marshall'st me the way that I was going;

And such an instrument I was to use.

Mine eyes are made the fools o' the other senses,

Or else worth all the rest; I see thee still,

And on thy blade and dudgeon gouts of blood,

Which was not so before. There's no such thing:

It is the bloody business which informs

Thus to mine eyes. . . .

. . . Thou sure and firm-set earth,

Hear not my steps, which way they walk, for fear

Thy very stones prate of my whereabout,

And take the present horror from the time,

Which now suits with it. Whiles I threat, he lives:

Words to the heat of deeds too cold breath gives.

If you are struggling to comprehend, see one of the sites listed below for a translation:
www.nosweatshakespeare.com/quotes/soliloquies/macbeth-dagger-before-me.htm
www.bardweb.net/content/readings/macbeth/lines.html

HANDOUT 2

IS THAT A _____ I SEE BEFORE ME?

Directions: On a separate piece of paper, you are going to write your own version of Macbeth's dagger soliloquy based on something that tempts you.

Your soliloquy must include the following:

1. At least three original lines from the text

2. An appeal to the senses

3. Two examples of figurative language

See my example below:

MACBETH

Is this a cupcake which I see before me,

The icing sticky and sweet? Come, let me clutch thee.

    Example of an appeal to senses (touch and taste)

I have thee not, and yet I see thee still.

Art thou not, fatal vision, sensible

To feeling as to sight? or art thou but

    Example of original text

A cupcake of the mind, a false creation,

Proceeding from my sugar craving stomach?

I see thee yet, in form as palpable

As this which I have baked.

Thou marshall'st me toward the kitchen;

Where salads green as grass I was to eat.

    Example #1 of figurative language

Mine eyes are made the fools o' the other senses,

Or else worth all the rest; I see thee still,

And on thy icing thousands of sprinkles,

Which was not so before. There's no such thing:

It is the hunger and sugar cravings which informs

Example #2 of figurative language.

Thus to mine eyes. . . .

. . . Thou sure and firm-set scales,

Hear not my steps, which way they walk, for fear

Thy very measures prate of my weight gain,

And take the present horror from the time,

Which now suits with it. Whiles I threat, the cupcake sits:

Words to the delight of taste too cold breath gives.

Lesson Plan Template

TOPIC:

Lincoln's Gettysburg Address (Grades 11–12)

CCSS STRAND:

Reading

TEXT TYPES AND PURPOSES:

Argue/Persuade

TIMING:

4 class periods

BACKWARD DESIGN COMPONENTS:

DESIRED RESULTS/CCSS ADDRESSED:

- Understand the meaning of the passage [R.1, R.2, R.3, R.10].

- Analyze the use of rhetorical strategies to present a convincing argument [R.4, R.5, R.6, L.3].

- Apply their understanding and analysis of Lincoln's rhetoric to the creation of a found poem [R.4, R.5, W.1].

- Compare speeches, and present their thoughts on how speeches of the past might influence current speechwriters [R.8, R.9, R.10, SL.4].

ACCEPTABLE EVIDENCE:

- Students' Found Poetry

- Students' speech analysis organizers

- Students' 150-word paragraph connecting previous presidential speeches with current speechwriters

LEARNING EXPERIENCES AND INSTRUCTION:

- Day 1—Brainstorm strong speech elements. Read and annotate Lincoln's Gettysburg Address. Create Found Poetry.

- Day 2—Compare Lincoln's style with Obama's style in his victory speech.

- Days 3–4—Share advice excerpts that have been gathered for homework.

STRATEGIES:

- Guidance and Monitoring
- Modeling
- Discussion

SUPPLEMENTAL RESOURCES:

- Simplified text (*READ* magazine)

TECHNOLOGY/MEDIA OPPORTUNITIES:

- Great American Speeches Website: www.americanrhetoric.com/ top100speechesall.html

SERVICE LEARNING LINK:

- Students could post inspirational quotes from the speeches in the school lobby, cafeteria, or gym.

- Students could use the speeches to help them advocate for a cause that matters to them by writing letters to politicians or to newspaper editors incorporating the rhetorical choices of the speechwriters.

VARIATIONS:

- Create interdisciplinary links by focusing on a particular historical era (SS), environmental issues (science), economics (SS, math), or international speeches in other languages (world languages).

- Review the closing statements for famous court cases. What rhetorical strategies did the lawyers use to present a strong argument?

LINCOLN'S GETTYSBURG ADDRESS

(Grades 11–12; Argue/Persuade)

Maureen Speaks

During our last presidential campaign, I witnessed a surge in my students' interest in politics. Students engaged in discussions about issues that mattered to them, but moreover, they analyzed and critiqued the major candidates. The media often compared Barack Obama with Abraham Lincoln, so I decided to dust off Lincoln's Gettysburg Address for formal analysis and for comparison with Obama's speeches [R.9, R.10]. When Obama won the election, and the world waited to see and hear what he would say on the day of his inauguration, my students and I delved into past speeches to solicit possible speech writing tips from men who had tackled this same daunting task of addressing the nation as U.S. president [R.4, R.5, R.6, L.3]. Since then, I use these lessons each year in January so that students will take an interest in the State of the Union address.

Materials Needed

Copy of the Gettysburg Address

Paper and pens

Handouts

Timing

4 class periods

Day 1—Brainstorm strong speech elements. Read and annotate Lincoln's Gettysburg Address. Create Found Poetry.

Day 2—Compare Lincoln's style with Obama's style in his victory speech.

Days 3–4—Share advice excerpts that have been gathered for homework.

It is ironic that Lincoln said, "The world will little note, nor long remember what we say here" because Lincoln's Gettysburg Address is arguably one of the most famous speeches in American history. If I say "Four score," my students' brains click into "and 7 years ago." The big question is, where do their brains go from there? Most do not know the next few words of the opening of this speech, let alone the context in which it was given. By participating in this lesson, I want students to get better acquainted with the text [R.1, R.2, R.3], appreciate the power and poetry of Lincoln's language [R.4, R.5, R.6, L.3], and demonstrate their understanding (orally and in writing) of how a strong model of public speaking like Lincoln can influence today's politicians or anyone writing a speech [R.8, R.9, R.10].

Day 1

I begin this unit by asking students to brainstorm elements of powerful speeches [R.4, R.5, R.6]. I ask them to think about plays and movies they may have seen that include moving speeches. I also ask them to think about any actual speeches they may have heard (political, keynote addresses, graduation speeches). Some common responses regarding elements of a good speech include

1. Connection with audience

2. Humor

3. Tone—not elitist

4. Repetition—anaphora

5. Exemplification

6. Diction—understandable but eloquent

7. Quotes/Allusions

8. Ethos/Logos/Pathos

9. Rhetorical Questions

10. Pauses

11. Sound bites—sentences or sections that can stand on their own

12. Content is important

Once we make this list, we are able to look at Lincoln's Gettysburg Address with a critical eye (**Handout 1**). We tackle the last thing on the list first [R.1, R.2, R.3, R.10]. Incidentally, I find it interesting that content is usually near the bottom of this list when I conduct this brainstorming. This year, I asked my students about this, and their response was that they assume the content is important if it is being publicized in a speech. Our reading for understanding supports students' assumption in the case of Lincoln's Gettysburg Address: Honoring the soldiers and encouraging listeners to further dedicate themselves to the cause of freedom for which the soldiers died seems important to them.

After understanding is established, we read again and look for some of the elements on our brainstorming list [R.4, R.5, R.6, L.3].

A helpful resource for this can be found in *READ* magazine. Lincoln's original speech is printed along with a more plainspoken rewrite of the speech ("Abraham Lincoln's Wonderful Way With Words," 2011). The meaning is the same in both works, so this juxtaposition clarifies how Lincoln's style made this speech a powerful document in American history.

 TECH CONNECTION: This is made easier when the speech is projected on an interactive white board. Annotations can easily be kept from day to day or posted on a website.

 DIFFERENTIATION TIP: With struggling learners, it may be best to start with the simplified version before moving into Lincoln's advanced rhetoric.

THEORY LINK (Bloom): Students are required to do more than *comprehend* basic meaning. They must *analyze* style.

THEORY LINK (Gardner): Appeals to Verbal-Linguistic and/or Visual-Spatial Intelligences.

DIFFERENTIATION TIP: Students may opt to work in pairs.

THEORY LINK (Dewey): Purposeful learning—students are becoming more advanced critical thinkers when it comes to politics and rhetoric. This logically leads to them being better-informed citizens.

TECH CONNECTION: If students e-mail their found poems to you, it is much easier to cut and paste the poems to post them on your class website.

THEORY LINK (Bloom): Again, students are required to do more than *comprehend* basic meaning. They must *analyze* how style supports the purpose of the speech.

Once this understanding of the importance of style is developed, students review some commentary on the speech and consider textual evidence that would support commentators on the speech [R.8, R.9, R.10] (**Handout 1**). I love Carl Sandburg's description of the address as "The great American poem." Based on this description, I ask students to create their own found poems using the text from the speech [R.4, R.5, W.1]. We discuss how modifying line endings and placement of text (without changing the actual language) highlights Lincoln's diction and phrasing. I provide a model for them (**Handout 1**). After that, students create their own found poems based on Lincoln's words.

For homework, students complete their found poems and begin exploring other presidential speeches that might be considered examples of powerful writing [R.8, R.9, R.10] (**Handout 2**). They must examine a more recent speech and an older speech, note rhetorical devices used by the author, and consider how choices in style and content might influence today's speechwriters. This will be shared on Day 3.

Day 2

We begin our second day by sharing poems using the ELMO projector if students bring in hard copies or by projectin e-mailed versions.

After reviewing students' poems and, therefore, Lincoln's language, we view Obama's November 2008 acceptance speech. I ask students to note any stylistic similarities between Lincoln's address and Obama's speech [R.4, R.5, R.6, L.3]. One very obvious similarity is the use of groupings of three to create rhythm (e.g., Lincoln's "We can not dedicate—we can not consecrate—we can not hallow" and Obama's "If there is anyone out there who still doubts . . . who still wonders . . . who still questions . . ."). They also note the use of allusion (Lincoln—"all men are created equal," Obama quotes Lincoln—"though passion may have strained it must not break our bonds of affection"). Also, they note figurative language (Lincoln's personification—"a new birth of freedom" and Obama's metaphor—"put their hands on the arc of history and bend it once more toward the hope of a better day"). Through this guided comparison, students become more confident in their analytical skills.

They then complete an organizer that calls for a simple thesis statement regarding the writing style and purpose of the speech, followed by textual evidence that supports the analysis (**Handout 3**) for Obama's speech. Doing this in class assures me that students are able to complete two more of the same organizers for the speeches of their choice, independently for days 3 and 4.

Days 3–4

Students e-mail to me portions of speeches that might be a good influence on Obama's speechwriters in terms of content and style. They share their findings with the class, referring to the graphic organizer and to their 150-word written statement [R.1, R.2, R.3, R.8, R.9, R.10, SL.4]. This usually takes approximately 2 days. Some students' choices overlap, so this saves time in reading excerpts. I am always very pleased with the way that this unit opens students' minds to a wide selection of presidential speeches and how it makes them more critical of the rhetoric put forth by today's politicians.

HANDOUT 1

LINCOLN'S GETTYSBURG ADDRESS

Gettysburg, Pennsylvania (November 19, 1863)

Four score and seven years ago our fathers brought forth on this continent, a new nation, conceived in Liberty, and dedicated to the proposition that all men are created equal.

Now we are engaged in a great civil war, testing whether that nation, or any nation so conceived and so dedicated, can long endure. We are met on a great battle-field of that war. We have come to dedicate a portion of that field, as a final resting place for those who here gave their lives that that nation might live. It is altogether fitting and proper that we should do this.

But, in a larger sense, we can not dedicate—we can not consecrate—we can not hallow—this ground. The brave men, living and dead, who struggled here, have consecrated it, far above our poor power to add or detract. The world will little note, nor long remember what we say here, but it can never forget what they did here. It is for us the living, rather, to be dedicated here to the unfinished work which they who fought here have thus far so nobly advanced. It is rather for us to be here dedicated to the great task remaining before us—that from these honored dead we take increased devotion to that cause for which they gave the last full measure of devotion—that we here highly resolve that these dead shall not have died in vain—that this nation, under God, shall have a new birth of freedom—and that government of the people, by the people, for the people, shall not perish from the earth.

Commentary:

On June 1, 1865, Senator Charles Sumner commented on what is now considered the most famous speech by President Abraham Lincoln. In his eulogy on the slain president, he called it a "monumental act." He said Lincoln was mistaken that "the world will little note, nor long remember what we say here." Rather, the Bostonian remarked, "The world noted at once what he said, and will never cease to remember it. The battle itself was less important than the speech."

The great American poem.

—*Carl Sandburg*

The ultimate expression of the majesty of Shakespeare's language.

—*Winston Churchill II*

SAMPLE FOUND POEM

Four score and seven years ago

our fathers brought forth on this continent,

a new nation,

conceived in Liberty,

and dedicated to the proposition that all men are created equal.

Now we are engaged in a great civil war,

testing whether that nation, or any nation so conceived and so dedicated,

can long endure.

We are met on a great battle-field of that war.

We have come to dedicate a portion of that field, as a final resting place

for those who here gave their lives that that nation might live.

It is altogether fitting and proper that we should do this.

HANDOUT 2

SPEECH UNIT—INDEPENDENT ASSIGNMENT

1. Read two State of the Union speeches (one from the past 50 years and another that is older).

2. Complete a rhetorical analysis page for each speech.

3. Choose one speech and write a 150-word response explaining how the style and content of the speech could influence Obama's State of the Union address.

4. E-mail to me (as an attachment and pasted into the body of the e-mail) AND PRINT a 100-word section of the speech by _____ night!

    Please format your e-mail in the following way:

    Your name _____

    President's name _____

    Year of the speech _____

    100-word section

5. Be prepared to discuss your excerpt with the class, using your 150-word response.

All work for this project will be graded according to the attached Grading Checklist.

SPEECH UNIT—INDEPENDENT ASSIGNMENT

Grading Checklist

Rhetorical Analysis Organizer 1 (25 points) _____

Speech _____

- All pertinent speech information is included
- Thesis links style and purpose
- Rhetorical devices are accurately labeled
- Discussion of the effect of the devices is clear and logical
- Link to the author's purpose (and your thesis) is clear and logical

23–25=excellent, 20–22=good, 18–19=fair, 16–17=poor, <16=failing

Rhetorical Analysis Organizer 2 (25 points) _____

Speech _____

- All pertinent speech information is included
- Thesis links style and purpose
- Rhetorical devices are accurately labeled
- Discussion of the effect of the devices is clear and logical
- Link to the author's purpose (and your thesis) is clear and logical

23–25=excellent, 20–22=good, 18–19=fair, 16–17=poor, <16=failing

150-Word Response (25 points) _____

Speech _____

- All pertinent speech information is included
- Logical *content-based* connection is made between the speech and the upcoming State of the Union address
- Logical *style* connection is made between the speech and the upcoming State of the Union address

23–25=excellent, 20–22=good, 18–19=fair, 16–17=poor, <16=failing

Presentation of Your Ideas (20 points) _____

- Well-organized
- Strong awareness of and comfort with content

- Good speaking skills (eye contact, posture, tone of voice)
- Strong ability to field questions from the audience

18–20=excellent, 16–17=good, 14–15=fair, 12–13=poor, <12=failing

Timeliness (5 points) _____

- All written elements are submitted on time.

5=excellent, 4=good, 3=fair, 2=poor, <1=failing

TOTAL _____

HANDOUT 3

RHETORICAL ANALYSIS ORGANIZER

Name _____

Speech Title _____

Speaker _____

Date _____

Context _____

Your Thesis _____

_____

(Tell how the style of the speech emphasizes the content or purpose)

Rhetorical Device 1: _____

Passage: _____

_____

Effect of Device: _____

_____

Link to author's rhetorical purpose (stated in your thesis):

_____

Rhetorical Device 2: _____

Passage: _____

_____

Effect of Device: _____

_____

Link to author's rhetorical purpose (stated in your thesis):

_____

Part II

Writing

4 The Benefits of CCSS for the Teaching of Writing

The time to begin writing an article is when you have finished it to your satisfaction. By that time you begin to clearly and logically perceive what it is you really want to say.

—Mark Twain

Writers are revisionists. When we engage in a literacy act, whether reading, writing, or speaking, we tend to want to go back and revise it in order to improve it. This is because we write in order to discover what we want to say; only after we have said it can we go back to try to express it better. This is the beauty of reading and writing: The act of discovery and the recursive nature of each allows us to go back and make changes to any part of the process. When writing about a topic, we can begin writing and then go back in the process to make changes in form or content. We can finish writing the draft and then realize that the introduction does not correspond well to the rest of the essay, and then write an entirely new introduction. With a word processor, we can cut or copy and paste and delete text, and even track changes to record our revisions. We can save our work and revisit it in the future.

The writing process approach that became popular in the 1970s is based on the idea that the steps of planning, drafting, revising, editing, and publishing (or simply prewriting, drafting, and rewriting) produce good writing. The goal is to produce a final draft (as *final* as time permits), after writing multiple drafts, appropriate to the topic, purpose, and audience. Writing for an authentic audience yields more realistic and effective writing. All modes of writing are respected and valued, including narrative and exploratory writing. In the classroom, students are encouraged to participate in the writing process and given multiple opportunities to practice improving their work. Prewriting activities, such as brainstorming and outlining, allow them to articulate their thoughts and design a plan. They conference with their peers and teacher during the rewriting stage, receive feedback, and work on editing and revising the meaning and form of their writing. They initiate their own writing and write about topics of their choice because, according to the approach, everybody has a story to tell.

The way some of us taught writing to our adolescent students using the process approach is different from the way we were taught writing through the product approach. As students, we were required to write one coherent, grammatically correct draft on an assigned topic usually in the format of an essay for a single audience, the teacher, in a single sitting. The teacher graded the essay and commented particularly on grammar and returned it to us without necessarily expecting a revised draft. There were limited opportunities for student input regarding topic, format, audience, and revision.

The product approach to writing, prevalent before the 1960s, emphasized formalism, correctness, and structure. It embraced grammar and mechanics and did not take into account students' meaning-making processes. The approach was based on the idea that teachers were the experts, filling knowledge in the empty vessels of students' brains. Students had nothing to offer and depended on teachers to supply them with the knowledge and skills necessary to succeed academically. Writing for exploration and discovery were not valued. The expository essay was the staple of school writing curriculum, and creative (expressive, poetic) writing took a back seat. This teacher-centered philosophy is contrary to the student-centeredness that characterizes much of the teaching and learning that take place in U.S. classrooms today.

The Common Core State Standards (CCSS) embrace both writing approaches (see Table 4.1.), and although they recognize the validity of narrative writing and creative self-expression, they also put a strong focus on the need for argumentative writing and the need to provide evidence to support claims about the text. In addition, students must engage in a range of writing across genres (appropriate to task, purpose, audience) and time frames (research project vs. writing on demand). After years of focusing on student self-expression, development of process writing, and traditional print-enhanced environment in English Language Arts (ELA) classrooms, the CCSS provide a balanced approach to expectations for writing that puts particular emphasis on various text types, especially argument, which has been neglected over the years, meaning as well as form, and the role of technology in enhancing writing.

In this chapter, we will introduce the CCSS for Writing and provide commentary on the value of each of the Anchor Standards for increasing student college and career readiness. We hope that by teaching to these standards, teachers will be able to help students write better. For easy reference, the

Anchor Standards for Writing that we will discuss throughout this chapter are listed in Table 4.1. At the end of the chapter, we will go beyond the general Anchor Standards and examine the 6–8, 9–10, and 11–12 grade-specific standards for "Research to Build and Present Knowledge."

Table 4.1	Anchor Standards for Writing (National Governors Association Center for Best Practices [NGA Center]/Council of Chief State School Officers [CCSSO], 2010b, p. 41)

Text Types and Purposes

1. Write arguments to support claims in an analysis of substantive topics or texts, using valid reasoning and relevant and sufficient evidence.

2. Write informative/explanatory texts to examine and convey complex ideas and information clearly and accurately through the effective selection, organization, and analysis of content.

3. Write narratives to develop real or imagined experiences or events using effective technique, well-chosen details, and well-structured event sequences.

Production and Distribution of Writing

4. Produce clear and coherent writing in which the development, organization, and style are appropriate to task, purpose, and audience.

5. Develop and strengthen writing as needed by planning, revising, editing, rewriting, or trying a new approach.

6. Use technology, including the Internet, to produce and publish writing and to interact and collaborate with others.

Research to Build and Present Knowledge

7. Conduct short as well as more sustained research projects based on focused questions, demonstrating understanding of the subject under investigation.

8. Gather relevant information from multiple print and digital sources, assess the credibility and accuracy of each source, and integrate the information while avoiding plagiarism.

9. Draw evidence from literary or informational texts to support analysis, reflection, and research.

Range of Writing

10. Write routinely over extended time frames (time for research, reflection, and revision) and shorter time frames (a single sitting or a day or two) for a range of tasks, purposes, and audiences.

TEXT TYPES AND PURPOSES

In a study conducted by Partnership for 21st Century Skills (2006) of employers' perspectives of high school graduates' workforce readiness, survey results indicated that 72% of employers thought that high school graduates are deficient in writing. The standards for "Text Types and Purposes" address the types of writing that students should be engaged in (argument, informative/explanatory, narrative) as well as the purposes for which they write (argue/persuade, inform/explain, convey experience). Many of the skills that students need to develop are transferable among text types and purposes. The CCSS for "Text Types and Purposes" are the following:

1. Write arguments to support claims in an analysis of substantive topics or texts, using valid reasoning and relevant and sufficient evidence.

2. Write informative/explanatory texts to examine and convey complex ideas and information clearly and accurately through the effective selection, organization, and analysis of content.

3. Write narratives to develop real or imagined experiences or events using effective technique, well-chosen details, and well-structured event sequences.

The CCSS call for students to become well-rounded individuals who write different types of texts (e.g., argument, informative, narrative) for different purposes and audiences. Writing for different purposes and audiences stimulates different kinds of thinking—logical, exploratory aesthetic, and expressive (Soven, 1999). Mastering all of these kinds of thinking leads to well-rounded individuals. Dewey would certainly approve of this idea that purposeful writing provides students with real-world, experiential learning that enhances their development as learners as well as individuals.

Stating arguments is common practice in the real world. Some children (including Vicky's) may argue with their parents about going to sleep at 8 p.m. When parents ask them why, they may offer arguments such as, "Grownups don't sleep this early." "But you're not in bed." "Emanuel's mom lets him sleep later." "I need to finish my homework." "Remember the time when I went to sleep at 10 p.m. and was fine the next day?" "I know sleep is good for you, but I personally do not need a lot of sleep." Some of these are compelling arguments that can lead to quite a battle; hopefully, parents' arguments are more reasonable ("because I say so" is not convincing enough, we're afraid).

The CCSS place special emphasis on writing logical arguments to prepare students to be college and career ready. Writing arguments to support claims by providing logical reasoning and strong, sufficient evidence is necessary for students' success in the world. How else will they be able to convince their professor that they deserve a higher grade in the course; or their employer that they deserve a raise; or their local councilman that building nuclear power plants in their neighborhood will increase the risk of cancer and other diseases and endanger people's lives?

According to the CCSS,

> Arguments are used for many purposes—to change the reader's point of view, to bring about some action on the reader's part, or to ask the reader to accept the writer's explanation or evaluation of a concept, issue, or problem. An argument is a reasoned, logical way of demonstrating that the writer's position, belief, or conclusion is valid. (NGA Center/CCSSO, 2010c, p. 23)

Writers consider two or more perspectives on an issue, think critically and deeply, assess the validity of these perspectives as well as their own thinking, and present the pros and cons while anticipating counterarguments. The levels of thinking range from basic recall to the more sophisticated stage of evaluation on Bloom's Taxonomy.

The CCSS for ELA make a point to clarify the distinction between argument and persuasive writing:

> When writing to persuade, writers employ a variety of persuasive strategies. One common strategy is an appeal to the credibility, character, or authority of the writer (or speaker). When writers establish that they are knowledgeable and trustworthy, audiences are more likely to believe what they say. Another is an appeal to the audience's self-interest, sense of identity, or emotions, any of which can sway an audience. A logical argument, on the other hand, convinces the audience because of the perceived merit and reasonableness of the claims and proofs offered rather than either the emotions the writing evokes in the audience or the character or credentials of the writer. (NGA Center/CCSSO, 2010c, p. 23)

For example, the argument that Paul should not go to sleep at 8 p.m. because his friend Emanuel gets to sleep later is reasonable; he makes a good point. Paul also brings up an opposing view, that although he recognizes the benefits of sleep, he personally, unlike other kids, does not need too much sleep. This evidence is logical, and so it would be considered argumentative by the CCSS. However, according to the CCSS, the rhetoric would be persuasive rather than argumentative if Paul were to present his case to his parents by focusing on his character: He could state that he has the maturity to make the decision regarding his own bedtime; after all, he has been behaving extremely well lately—helping out in the house: making his bed, picking up his toys; earning an "A" on his math test; and so on. Paul could also be persuasive by appealing to his parents' emotions by saying that he loves his parents very much.

Argumentative devices could also be used in narrative structures. The CCSS expect students to write narratives about real or imagined experience using effective devices, details, and logical progression of events. The purposes for these narratives include to "inform, instruct, persuade, or entertain" (NGA Center/CCSSO, 2010c, p. 23). Narrative forms may include memoirs, fictional stories, autobiographies, and other genres.

Contrary to argument and narrative, the purpose of informative/exploratory texts is to advance a reader's knowledge or comprehension about a subject. Even though informative elements are included in argument and narrative, informative/explanatory writing is used for clarification. In this type of writing, students convey intricate ideas through the accurate and clear use of content. Genres include literary analyses, reports, summaries, and real workplace functional writing, such as memos, applications, and so on (NGA Center/CCSSO, 2010c).

PRODUCTION AND DISTRIBUTION OF WRITING

According to the Partnership for 21st Century Skills (2006), 62.8% of employers surveyed reported that high school graduates' technology skills are "adequate." However, given that 72% of those employers stated that students are deficient in writing, clearly, students need to learn how to apply their technology skills to improve their writing. The CCSS for "Production and Distribution of Writing" address the components of well-written work (development, organization, style), the process of creating high quality work (planning, revising, editing), and utilizing technology to publish writing:

4. Produce clear and coherent writing in which the development, organization, and style are appropriate to task, purpose, and audience.

5. Develop and strengthen writing as needed by planning, revising, editing, rewriting, or trying a new approach.

6. Use technology, including the Internet, to produce and publish writing and to interact and collaborate with others.

According to the *Framework for Success in Postsecondary Writing* (The Council of Writing Program Administrators [CWPA], the National Council of Teachers of English [NCTE], and the National Writing Project [NWP], 2011), "Rhetorical knowledge is the ability to analyze and act on understandings of audiences, purposes, and contexts in creating and comprehending texts . . . . By developing rhetorical knowledge, writers can adapt to different purposes, audiences, and contexts" (p. 10). This flexibility of composing is essential for good writing as writers learn to compose for different tasks and purposes. According to the CCSS, students are expected to produce clear writing appropriate to task, purpose, and audience. They engage in the writing process as needed. They can go back to any step of the composing process that will help advance their writing. Technology can help students produce and publish their writing. They can use the word processor to compose or create a wiki to post information or a blog to offer opinions about a topic. They can analyze and evaluate electronic sources and incorporate them in their writing and examine how technology affects a piece of writing.

Software programs, such as Microsoft Print Shop and Publisher, provide templates and graphic development tools to help users create projects, such as brochures, newsletters, and so on.

Students also use this technology to interact and communicate with others. They can use the above applications to learn collaboratively. Many of the software allow users to create projects within a shared interface. Social media, such as Facebook, could be used to share information about literary and informational texts and persuade users to accept a particular point of view. Applying Gardner's theory, learners with Interpersonal Intelligence benefit from the use of technology in writing.

RESEARCH TO BUILD AND PRESENT KNOWLEDGE

Never has the act of conducting research been easier than today with the Internet at our fingertips. If you have a question (about anything), you can Google (which has become a verb) to find the answer. When you Google the keyword "metaphor," you get 33.7 million results. This is wonderful for students nowadays seeking information about metaphor but overwhelming because of the enormous number of websites at their disposal. It has never been more important than the present for students to learn to assess the credibility and accuracy of each electronic source of information without plagiarizing before integrating it into their writing. The CCSS for "Research to Build and Present Knowledge" address the need for students to make their research accurate and inclusive of varied sources.

7. Conduct short as well as more sustained research projects based on focused questions, demonstrating understanding of the subject under investigation.

8. Gather relevant information from multiple print and digital sources, assess the credibility and accuracy of each source, and integrate the information while avoiding plagiarism.

9. Draw evidence from literary or informational texts to support analysis, reflection, and research.

According to the CCSS, students must research and gather information from various print and electronic sources and synthesize it coherently. The research should be short-term as well as long-term. Students need to be able to be flexible in gathering and understanding information from research over a short period of time as well as a longer time frame.

In addition, students must also draw evidence from literary and informational texts to support their research, analysis, and reflection. Providing supporting proof from text makes ideas and information credible and valid.

For example, a teacher assigns students to read about and analyze information regarding recent budget cuts in physical education classes from print and digital informational sources, and write a letter to the governor to persuade him to reduce or increase spending in the area of fitness in schools. In their letters, students must explain clearly in writing their position supported by evidence from the informational sources in order to persuade the governor to take a particular course of action. The textual evidence is essential in establishing the credibility of the writer and appealing to the reader's "self-interest, sense of identity, or emotions" (NGA Center/CCSSO, 2010c, p. 24).

RANGE OF WRITING

It is necessary in this era of testing that requires timed written responses (short answer, e.g., paragraph; or extended response, e.g., essay) that students meet Standard 10:

> 10. Write routinely over extended time frames (time for research, reflection, and revision) and shorter time frames (a single sitting or a day or two) for a range of tasks, purposes, and audiences.

Students need to be able to write within time constraints. For example, they may be asked to write an essay in as little as 20 minutes or produce a 10-page paper by the end of the week. Communicating effectively also applies to texting, e-mail, Twitter, blogging, and other electronic modes of communication, where even though the language may be unique to the mode, the intended message still needs to get across. An awareness of audience is also still important. (The reader can imagine Vicky's disappointment when her graduate students send her e-mails regarding the course with texting language, acronyms, and no punctuation or capitalization, let alone a salutation or signature.)

Success in the real world depends on the ability of students to write flexibly. Workplace functions include completing a job application, writing a memo, and composing a letter. College expectations include writing short responses, longer responses, and more sustained projects (e.g., papers, reports) in various genres, including creative writing, literary analyses, scientific or historical reports, and summaries. Writing depending on what the situation calls for is an essential aspect of college and career readiness.

A CLOSER LOOK

Let's look at the grade-specific standards for the first set of standards under "Research to Build and Present Knowledge" for Grades 6–12 to determine what students need to be able to know and do by the end of each grade band (see Tables 4.2 and 4.3). In Grade 6, students "conduct short research projects to

Table 4.2   Writing Standards 6–8 (NGA Center/CCSSO, 2010b, p. 44)

Grade 6 Students	Grade 7 Students	Grade 8 Students
Research to Build and Present Knowledge	*Research to Build and Present Knowledge*	*Research to Build and Present Knowledge*
7. Conduct short research projects to answer a question, drawing on several sources and refocusing the inquiry when appropriate.	7. Conduct short research projects to answer a question, drawing on several sources and generating additional related, focused questions for further research and investigation.	7. Conduct short research projects to answer a question (including a self-generated question), drawing on several sources and generating additional related, focused questions that allow for multiple avenues of exploration.
8. Gather relevant information from multiple print and digital sources; assess the credibility of each source; and quote or paraphrase the data and conclusions of others while avoiding plagiarism and providing basic bibliographic information for sources.	8. Gather relevant information from multiple print and digital sources, using search terms effectively; assess the credibility and accuracy of each source; and quote or paraphrase the data and conclusions of others while avoiding plagiarism and following a standard format for citation.	8. Gather relevant information from multiple print and digital sources, using search terms effectively; assess the credibility and accuracy of each source; and quote or paraphrase the data and conclusions of others while avoiding plagiarism and following a standard format for citation.
9. Draw evidence from literary or informational texts to support analysis, reflection, and research. a. Apply *Grade 6 Reading standards* to literature (e.g., "Compare and contrast texts in different forms or genres [e.g., stories and poems; historical novels and fantasy stories] in terms of their approaches to similar themes and topics"). b. Apply *Grade 6 Reading standards* to literary nonfiction (e.g., "Trace and evaluate the argument and specific claims in a text, distinguishing claims that are supported by reasons and evidence from claims that are not").	9. Draw evidence from literary or informational texts to support analysis, reflection, and research. a. Apply *Grade 7 Reading standards* to literature (e.g., "Compare and contrast a fictional portrayal of a time, place, or character and a historical account of the same period as a means of understanding how authors of fiction use or alter history"). b. Apply *Grade 7 Reading standards* to literary nonfiction (e.g., "Trace and evaluate the argument and specific claims in a text, assessing whether the reasoning is sound and the evidence is relevant and sufficient to support the claims").	9. Draw evidence from literary or informational texts to support analysis, reflection, and research. a. Apply *Grade 8 Reading standards* to literature (e.g., "Analyze how a modern work of fiction draws on themes, patterns of events, or character types from myths, traditional stories, or religious works such as the Bible, including describing how the material is rendered new"). b. Apply *Grade 8 Reading standards* to literary nonfiction (e.g., "Delineate and evaluate the argument and specific claims in a text, assessing whether the reasoning is sound and the evidence is relevant and sufficient; recognize when irrelevant evidence is introduced").

Table 4.3   Writing Standards 9–12 (NGA Center/CCSSO, 2010b, p. 47)

Grades 9–10 Students	Grades 11–12 Students
Research to Build and Present Knowledge	*Research to Build and Present Knowledge*
7. Conduct short as well as more sustained research projects to answer a question (including a self-generated question) or solve a problem; narrow or broaden the inquiry when appropriate; synthesize multiple sources on the subject, demonstrating understanding of the subject under investigation.	**7.** Conduct short as well as more sustained research projects to answer a question (including a self-generated question) or solve a problem; narrow or broaden the inquiry when appropriate; synthesize multiple sources on the subject, demonstrating understanding of the subject under investigation.
8. Gather relevant information from multiple authoritative print and digital sources, using advanced searches effectively; assess the usefulness of each source in answering the research question; integrate information into the text selectively to maintain the flow of ideas, avoiding plagiarism and following a standard format for citation.	**8.** Gather relevant information from multiple authoritative print and digital sources, using advanced searches effectively; assess the strengths and limitations of each source in terms of the task, purpose, and audience; integrate information into the text selectively to maintain the flow of ideas, avoiding plagiarism and overreliance on any one source and following a standard format for citation.
9. Draw evidence from literary or informational texts to support analysis, reflection, and research. a. Apply *Grades 9–10 Reading standards* to literature (e.g., "Analyze how an author draws on and transforms source material in a specific work [e.g., how Shakespeare treats a theme or topic from Ovid or the Bible or how a later author draws on a play by Shakespeare]"). b. Apply *Grades 9–10 Reading standards* to literary nonfiction (e.g., "Delineate and evaluate the argument and specific claims in a text, assessing whether the reasoning is valid and the evidence is relevant and sufficient; identify false statements and fallacious reasoning").	**9.** Draw evidence from literary or informational texts to support analysis, reflection, and research. a. Apply *Grades 11–12 Reading standards* to literature (e.g., "Demonstrate knowledge of eighteenth-, nineteenth-, and early-twentieth-century foundational works of American literature, including how two or more texts from the same period treat similar themes or topics"). b. Apply *Grades 11–12 Reading standards* to literary nonfiction (e.g., "Delineate and evaluate the reasoning in seminal U.S. texts, including the application of constitutional principles and use of legal reasoning [e.g., in U.S. Supreme Court Case majority opinions and dissents] and the premises, purposes, and arguments in works of public advocacy [e.g., *The Federalist*, presidential addresses]").

answer a teacher-assigned question, drawing on several sources and refocusing the inquiry when appropriate." In Grade 7, students also conduct short research projects not only to answer the question but also to generate more questions for investigation. In Grade 8, students conduct short research projects to answer a teacher-assigned question (as well as a self-generated one) and generate more questions that allow for *multiple avenues of exploration.* Researching and generating questions for investigation that allow for multiple avenues (print, digital) is the higher expectation. The Grades 9–10 and 11–12 standards are identical: Students

> conduct short as well as more sustained research projects to answer a question (including a self-generated question) or solve a problem; narrow or broaden the inquiry when appropriate; synthesize multiple sources on the subject, demonstrating understanding of the subject under investigation. (NGA/CCSSO, 2010b, p. 46)

Whereas in the lower grades they research questions (whether teacher generated in Grades 6–7 or self-generated in Grade 8) using a single avenue (Grades 6–7) or multiple avenues (Grade 8), in the higher grades (9–12), they take an additional step and synthesize multiple sources for investigation.

In terms of gathering information, in Grade 6, students "Gather relevant information from multiple print and digital sources; assess the credibility of each source; and quote or paraphrase the data and conclusions of others while avoiding plagiarism and providing basic bibliographic information for sources"; in Grade 7, they gather the information using search terms effectively and assess not only the credibility but also the accuracy of each source and follow a standard format of citation (e.g., Modern Language Association or American Psychological Association); in Grade 8, they follow identical expectations defined in Grade 7. Regarding drawing evidence, in all Grades 6–12, "Students draw evidence from literary or informational texts to support analysis, reflection, and research." Grade-specific reading standards for literature apply to these grade levels. The standard for "Range of Writing" is identical for all Grades 6–12: "Students write routinely over extended time frames (time for research, reflection, and revision) and shorter time frames (a single sitting or a day or two) for a range of tasks, purposes, and audiences."

CONCLUSION

There are three main points we think that the CCSS make regarding writing. First, the CCSS balance the process and product approaches to writing: Students produce writing for longer time frames (projects) supported by the steps of process writing as needed as well as shorter time frames (writing on demand). Expository essays are valued and so is exploratory writing for personal growth. Both meaning and form are central to good writing. Second, the CCSS emphasize the importance of using textual evidence necessary to support a writer's analysis, reflection, and research. Students write different pieces (argument, informative, narrative) for various purposes and audiences and when making claims must provide evidence from varied sources that influence their ideas. Last, the CCSS incorporate the use of technology as a means to produce and publish writing independently and in collaboration. Technology enhances writing, permitting multiple modes of exploration and communication.

Vicky had a student once, Alejandro, who was a good writer in his native Spanish language but had weak writing skills in English. His paragraphs were elaborate; his sentences were long with many clauses. In addition, there was a lack of immediate progression of ideas. In Spanish, his prose would probably be coherent, but in English there was a lack of coherence and focus. In Vicky's class, Alejandro practiced writing about multiple tasks and for various purposes and audiences. Vicky and Alejandro worked on initially getting the content out (which he had no problem doing) and then shaping the ideas into a coherent structure. Alejandro was more successful at writing narratives; however, he struggled with expository writing. He developed stories about growing up in Ecuador and his experiences in the United States. Vicky used his facility in writing about personal experience as a resource and tried to help him transfer his knowledge and skills regarding narrative writing to developing fluency in other types of writing (e.g., expository, persuasive/argumentative).

Alejandro used technology to enhance his writing, such as working on the word processor, which has spell and grammar check features, searching the Internet for information, and using blogs to post texts and communicate with classmates. He practiced prewriting, drafting, and rewriting in order to scaffold his composing but also completed timed writing activities to prepare for writing on demand tasks.

Alejandro was hard-working. He encountered frustration when he "just couldn't get it right." He made progress by the end of the year and performed relatively well on the state exam. More important than his exam score is that he developed an understanding of the ongoing process of developing his writing skills. Alejandro would not consider himself a success story; he considered himself a work in progress. Though Alejandro might have perceived passing his exam as a time to celebrate success, like Twain, he saw it as a time to "begin to clearly and logically perceive" how to expand his skills so as to write what it was that he really wanted to say. Do you have students like Alejandro? If so, how do you help them succeed in writing? How do you help them recognize their perceived "completion" of a writing piece as a place to start revising? How can the CCSS help?

QUESTIONS/CHALLENGES/ PONDERING POINTS

1. How has the 21st century changed your perspective on teaching writing?

2. How complex are the writing tasks that you are assigning to your students?

3. In what ways do your students need to improve their writing skills?

4. How do you design curriculum that addresses your students' needs for improvement in writing?

5. How does your instruction promote the development of students' writing skills?

5 Writing Lessons From the Classroom

INTRODUCTION

In this chapter, we will present three lessons that we believe are particularly effective for addressing the Common Core State Standards (CCSS) for Writing. In the Grades 6–8 lesson, Argument Rotation, students learn through collaboration how to construct effective arguments. The second lesson, Cyberbullying Letters, appropriate for Grades 9–10, focuses on synthesizing information from research to compose letters that advocate for cyberbullying prevention. Lastly, in the Grades 11–12 lesson, *This American Life*, students use information that they gather from interviews and other research to compose a multimodal story.

Within the first lesson, Argument Rotation, we examine the logical structure of argument and effective rhetorical approaches to forming a good argument. Students write an evidence-based argument essay. In the second lesson, Cyberbullying Letters, students analyze how characters and events in *The Chocolate War* develop and how they are shaped by the author's point of view. They research articles about cyberbullying and then use the information that they gather to write letters to preservice teachers explaining what they could do to prevent cyberbullying in their classrooms. This lesson combines literary and informational texts. *This American Life* requires students to examine effective storytelling devices modeled by the radio program *This American Life* and incorporating them into their Photo Stories. This is a multimodal assignment that stimulates students' thinking in multiple ways. In all three lessons, students learn to write for an appropriate task, purpose, and audience in an appropriate format. In the first lesson, they write to assert and defend claims; in the second, they write what they know about a topic; and in the third, they convey what they or others have experienced. They gather information, analyze it, and report it in a coherent way. They are given opportunities to revisit and make improvements to their writing.

As you read through these lessons and as you develop your own lessons, we encourage you to focus on how you can guide your students to meet the CCSS for Writing. Two sets of questions for reflection are listed below—specific questions pertaining to Writing Anchor Standards and general questions regarding Lesson Design.

WRITING ANCHOR STANDARDS REFLECTIVE QUESTIONS

How does the lesson require students to do one or more of the following?

1. Write arguments to support claims using valid reasoning and relevant and sufficient evidence?

2. Write informative/explanatory texts to examine and convey complex ideas and information clearly and accurately?

3. Write narratives to develop real or imagined experiences or events using effective technique, well-chosen details, and well-structured event sequences?

4. Produce clear and coherent writing appropriate to task, purpose, and audience?

5. Develop and strengthen writing as needed by planning, revising, editing, rewriting, or trying a new approach?

6. Use technology, including the Internet, to produce and publish writing and to collaborate with others?

7. Conduct short as well as more sustained research projects based on focused questions?

8. Gather relevant information from multiple print and digital sources, assess the sources, and synthesize the information without plagiarizing?

9. Draw evidence from literary or informational texts to support analysis, reflection, and research?

10. Write routinely over extended time frames and shorter time frames for a range of tasks, purposes, and audiences?

LESSON DESIGN REFLECTIVE QUESTIONS

1. How does the lesson require close and multiple readings of grade-level complex text (classic, contemporary, or informational)?

2. How does my questioning require students to use the text as support for their interpretations/arguments?

3. How does the lesson incorporate varied thinking skills (e.g., read, summarize, analyze, interpret)? (Bloom)

4. How does the lesson include the three components of Backward Design: (a) desired results, (b) acceptable evidence, and (c) learning experiences?

5. How do I differentiate instruction, materials, and expectations for this particular lesson so that struggling students can be successful?

6. How does the lesson provide opportunities for technology/media use?

7. How does the lesson include research-based instructional strategies to promote effective teaching?

8. How can the lesson present opportunities for interdisciplinary connections?

9. How does the lesson provide opportunities for students with varied Multiple Intelligences to be successful? (Gardner)

10. How do I present the lesson in a way that encourages students to see the value of what they are learning (e.g., service learning, college- and career-readiness skills)? (Dewey)

Lesson Plan Template

TOPIC:
Argument Rotation (Grades 6–8)

TEXT TYPES AND PURPOSES:
Argue/Persuade

CCSS STRAND:
Writing

TIMING:
3 class periods

BACKWARD DESIGN COMPONENTS:

DESIRED RESULTS/CCSS ADDRESSED:

- Demonstrate an understanding of logical argument structure and effective rhetorical approaches to forming an argument [R.8].

- Engage in process writing of argument essay [W.5].

- Compose a coherent argument essay in a timed setting [W.1, W.4, W.10].

- Use technology to celebrate student work [W.6].

ACCEPTABLE EVIDENCE:

- Rotating Argument Notes (Handout 1)

- Argument Essay

LEARNING EXPERIENCES AND INSTRUCTION:

- Day 1—Complete Rotating Argument Organizer.

- Day 2—Write argument essay.

- Day 3—Analyze and highlight strong points in student writing/Academy Awards.

STRATEGIES:

- Guidance and Monitoring
- Cooperative Learning
- Discussion
- Writing Process

SUPPLEMENTAL RESOURCES:

- List of Issues and Controversies (www .procon.org)

TECHNOLOGY/MEDIA OPPORTUNITIES:

- Students may post their arguments on a blog and invite others to comment.

SERVICE LEARNING LINK:

- Student may debate local, national, or global issues in their argument essays and investigate which organizations are working to address said issues. Based on student essays, the class may opt to adopt a cause.

VARIATIONS:

- Pair students and have them write from opposing viewpoints based on the topic.

- Allow students to brainstorm their own list of topics.

ARGUMENT ROTATION

(Grades 6–8; Argue/Persuade)

Vicky and Maureen Speak

Teenagers love to argue. This is clearly seen on any given day, in any given classroom. As their critical thinking skills are developed, so is their critical questioning of the world. One of our responsibilities as teachers is to help students hone their skills when it comes to presenting an argument effectively and fairly.

We all feel passionately about certain topics, but our passion does not ensure a logical format for arguing said topics. What if, as we were arguing, we were forced to pause and reflect on the argument as developed at that pause-point before moving on with our case? Most likely, such a practice would strengthen our line of thinking. In the real world, it is difficult to take time to pause while posing an argument. Passion and the desire to just get that person who is listening to come onto our side drives our arguments with speed and force that we may look back on with regret or, if we're lucky, wonder. This activity creates a habit of reflection for our students.

Materials Needed

Polling System: Classroom Response System or Student Response System or polleverywhere.com

Paper and pens

Handouts

Timing

3 class periods

Day 1—Complete Rotating Argument Organizers.

Day 2—Write argument essay.

Day 3—Analyze and highlight strong points in student writing/Academy Awards.

Day 1

THEORY LINK (Gardner): Appeals to Interpersonal Intelligence.

To begin this activity, students must be seated in groups of three. This is the ideal number for a 40-minute period. Each member of the group is given a different controversial topic and told to write a thesis statement based on his or her stance on that topic.

Some topics may include the following:

1. Should parents read their kids' e-mails?

2. Is it ethical to withhold treatment believed to help in order to have a control for a scientific study?

3. Is it OK to tell a white lie on a job application?

The topics above were debated at the 2011 Long Island Ethics Bowl. Other topics are available at www.bedfordstmartins.com/patterns under "Debate Topics." After students write their thesis statement, they are provided with an explanation of Toulmin's Argument Structure (**Handout 1**) and an organizer with basic components to include in their thesis and in their overall argument structure (**Handout 2**).

Once students have written their thesis statement, they begin Minor Claim 1 on the organizer. Most students expand on the grounds for their argument or jump right into a description of the action/change that they are advocating. After Minor Claim 1 is written, each student rotates his or her page to another group member to review and to build upon. The other group member writes Minor Claim 2, and a third group member writes a Counterargument. Group members can make slight changes, if needed, but cannot change the stance or the overall tone of the argument. Rather, regardless of opinion or belief, the student must continue to build a strong argument. This is often very interesting for students who do not necessarily agree with the thesis they are trying to defend. Said students often write a form of counterargument and address the faults within their own beliefs. This honesty and insight are often quite strong. The "Final Knockout Punch" is returned to the original writer on the organizer who must consider how peers have developed the line of reasoning and how to leave the readers of the essay.

We discuss the process as a class at the end of the period and decide if the introduction would need altering. We also discuss how to formulate a conclusion beyond the typical summarizing of topic sentence (for instance, including that "Final Knockout Punch"). Students realize what points in the arguments are strong when they share their writing with their peers [W.5]. This often leads to that powerful thoughtful rhetorical question or appeal to pathos that makes for a strong conclusion. Discussion of content and style is not limited to the conclusion. We brainstorm rhetorical devices that make an argument essay effective such as the use of three (I have not, I cannot, I will not), rhetorical questions (Would you be able to live with yourself if you had done this?), parallel structure (Making good choices cultivates joy. Making poor choices cultivates sorrow.), and repetition (I ask you, how can you live without joy? I ask you, how can anyone live without joy? I ask you, why would we make any choices that could diminish their joy?) [R.8].

THEORY LINK (Bloom): Students *analyze* and *evaluate* arguments.

Day 2

When students arrive for class, they reach into a grab bag with the three completed organizers for their groups, and based on the organizers that they pull, they are randomly assigned a topic from Day 1 on which to write an

DIFFERENTIATION TIP: Students can finish writing and even typing up their essays at home.

THEORY LINK (Gardner): Appeals to Verbal-Linguistic Intelligence.

THEORY LINK (Dewey): Purposeful learning— Students write for a real audience.

THEORY LINK (Gardner): Appeals to Bodily-Kinesthetic Intelligence.

THEORY LINK (Bloom): Students *evaluate* their peers' argumentative essays.

TECH CONNECTION: Students vote for their favorite using technology.

argumentative essay [W.1, W.4, W.10]. This essay will be assessed based on a grading checklist that is distributed at this time as well (**Handout 3**). Students are familiar with the topics because of the previous day's activity. Some students have reflected on the topics overnight and are particularly pleased when they pull a topic that was interesting to them. For instance, a student who is a fan of *Grey's Anatomy* may be thrilled to pull the topic of medical research and placebos.

Students bring their essays to class and share with their peers.

Day 3

This is the day for the Academy Awards where students' work is celebrated. The focus is more on content and style and the positive choices students have made in terms of argument rather than mechanics. Some of the categories include "Best Startling Fact" and "Best Rhetorical Question." Students vote for each category, and the teacher polls students' responses (using clicker or nonclicker systems, e.g., polleverywhere.com) [W.6].

A discussion ensues about what makes an argument effective and how to develop future essays. Also, students may make suggestions for future argument topics for this activity.

This activity is popular with students because of their love of arguing and questioning. The value in it is that it encourages students to be more reflective and to produce coherent, well-structured, evidence-based arguments.

HANDOUT 1

TOULMIN'S ADVICE FOR HOW TO CONSTRUCT AN ARGUMENT

Claim—This is what you believe and what you want your readers to believe.

Example:

I believe that students should be issued laptops instead of textbooks.

Grounds—Data or facts on which your claim is based.

Example:

Books cannot be updated as easily as online information. Also, the cost of one laptop per student is comparable to seven or eight textbooks over the course of 4 years.

Warrant—Connects claim and grounds.

Example:

Schools are concerned with providing up-to-date education that is cost-effective.

Counterargument—Addresses what a person may say to the contrary of your argument.

1. **Concede—note the potential disagreement/argument against your stance.**

2. **Refute—minimize the argument against your stance by telling how it is ineffective or how key players might address the issue raised.**

Example:

Some might argue that laptops create too much temptation for students to check e-mail or play games rather than focus on the teacher. [Concede]

However, schools can use software to block distracting sites; besides, students today are drawn to technology and will appreciate teachers' attempts to teach to their learning style. [Refute]

Adapted from http://changingminds.org/disciplines/argument/making_argument/toulmin.htm.

HANDOUT 2

ROTATING ARGUMENT—ORGANIZER

Topic _____

Thesis (include grounds, major claim, and warrant)

_____

_____

Minor Claim 1 (combine grounds, claim, warrant)

_____

_____

Minor Claim 2 (combine grounds, claim, warrant)

_____

_____

Counterargument (concede and refute)

_____

_____

"Final Knockout Punch" for conclusion

_____

_____

HANDOUT 3

ROTATING ARGUMENT ESSAY—GRADING CHECKLIST

Introduction (20 Points) _____

- – grabber
- – thesis includes grounds, claim, and warrant

  18–20=excellent, 16–17=good, 14–15=fair, 12–13=poor, <12=failing

Development (50 points) _____

- – additional supportive claims/evidence clearly relate to the main claim
- – includes a well-considered and well-developed counterargument
- – accurate
- – logical
- – effective use of rhetorical devices

  45–50=excellent, 40–44=good, 35–39=fair, 33–34=poor, <33=failing

Organization (20 points) _____

- – strong topic sentences
- – logical paragraph breakdown
- – clear conclusion
- – effective use of transitions

  18–20=excellent, 16–17=good, 14–15=fair, 12–13=poor, <12=failing

Mechanics and Readability (10 points) _____

- – spelling
- – punctuation
- – grammar
- – verb tense
- – overall fluency

  9–10=excellent, 8=good, 7=fair, 6=poor, <6=failing

  TOTAL_____

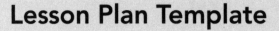

Lesson Plan Template

TOPIC:
Cyberbullying Letters (Grades 9–10)

CCSS STRAND:
Writing

TEXT TYPES AND PURPOSES:
Explain/Inform

TIMING:
4 class periods

BACKWARD DESIGN COMPONENTS:

DESIRED RESULTS/CCSS ADDRESSED:

- Analyze how characters and events in *The Chocolate War* develop and how the author's point of view shapes the content of the novel [R.3, R.6].

- Explain/inform reader about cyberbullying [W.2].

- Produce a clear and coherent research-based letter about cyberbullying that is appropriate for the audience of preservice teachers [W.4, W.7, W.8, W.9].

- Explain how cyberbullying applies to them by participating in the writing process in order to create their letters [W.5].

ACCEPTABLE EVIDENCE:

- Note cards, organizer, drafting
- Students' research-based letters

LEARNING EXPERIENCES AND INSTRUCTION:

- Day 1—Discuss the ending of *The Chocolate War.*
- Day 2—Introduce cyberbullying research.
- Day 3—Complete letter organizer and draft letter.
- Day 4—Share, peer-response, revise, publish.

STRATEGIES:

- Guidance and Monitoring
- Discussion
- Cooperative Learning
- Writing Process

SUPPLEMENTAL RESOURCES:

- Simplified articles on cyberbullying

TECHNOLOGY/MEDIA OPPORTUNITIES:

- CNN Video about Megan Meier (www .youtube.com/watch?v= HFsfDLCkfQU)

- It Gets Better Project site (www .itgetsbetter.org)

SERVICE LEARNING LINK:

- Students write letters to their peers regarding how to handle cyberbullying.

- Students hold a panel discussion with parents, teachers, administrators, and peers on the topic.

- Students create cyberbullying brochures for Parent Night.

VARIATIONS:

- Use with other issues that students are facing—drug/alcohol use, safe driving, time management.

- Preservice teachers brainstorm a list of topics that they would like to learn more about. Students create research-based letters on said topics.

CYBERBULLYING LETTERS

(Grades 9–10; Explain/Inform)

Maureen Speaks

I believe it is important to make clear connections between major themes addressed in literature and social issues that students face, thus providing the answer to that dreaded question: "Why do we have to read this?" *The Chocolate War* provides an excellent starting point for a conversation with students about bullying. Though the book focuses on face-to face bullying, I have found that most students are concerned with cyberbullying.

Materials Needed

Copy of *The Chocolate War*

Computers, Internet access

Paper and pens

Handouts

Timing

4 class periods

Day 1—Discuss the ending of *The Chocolate War.*

Day 2—Introduce cyberbullying research.

Day 3—Complete letter organizer and draft letter.

Day 4—Share, peer-response, revise, publish.

One example of thematic connections with students' lives stems from our reading of *The Chocolate War.* This novel is about a freshman boy who faces the tyranny of a group of school bullies called The Vigils. The Vigils are able to control their peers through intimidation and, at times, violence. What is most frightening regarding this group is that they operate with the silent approval of the school's headmaster. Also, most teachers know that the group exists, but there is a silent understanding that there is nothing to be done about these bullies. Though this book is a great fit for the discussion of bullying and the question of what authority figures should do about this issue, there are many other books that connect with this topic such as *Animal Farm, The Cage, Macbeth,* and *Romeo and Juliet.*

 DIFFERENTIATION TIP: Differentiation of materials.

Day 1

When we finish reading *The Chocolate War,* I ask students what they think the author, Robert Cormier, hoped we would learn from his novel. The students latch onto an allusion made to T.S. Eliot's "The Love Song of J. Alfred Prufrock," in which the main character asks, "Do I dare disturb the universe?"

In the novel, Jerry, the main character, asks himself the same thing. Does he dare to go against the bullies? Can he successfully change the way the school runs by defying the authority of The Vigils? When he tries, he is met with disastrous ends. I ask the students how they feel about this and usually hear something like "It's so depressing" or "Why does Cormier tell us to give up?"

With some further discussion of the difference between mood and tone (guided by **Handout 1**), the students realize that Cormier wants the reader to feel frustration when Jerry is defeated [R.3, R.6]. Though Jerry is telling his friend to conform at the end of the novel, Cormier hopes that the reader will be saying "No! Don't give up!" The most important thing to come out of this discussion is that we should not accept injustice. We should "disturb the universe" by taking action [R.3].

Day 2

I provide the students with an avenue for creating change by writing letters to preservice teachers cautioning them about student bullying [W.2]. Since the willingness of the teachers in the novel to turn their heads the other way regarding The Vigils in particular bothers the students, this is a writing activity

for which they are fairly motivated. To increase motivation, I provide students with information on cyberbullying (**Handout 2**).

This is an issue that students contend with on a daily basis. It is interesting to note that many do not realize that they are being cyberbullied or that they are cyberbullying others until they read some articles on the subject [W.7, W.8, W.9]. The most upsetting articles for the students are those about Megan Meier, a young girl who died by suicide because of the cyberbullying executed by the parent of a peer.

Day 3

Once the students read articles on what cyberbullying is, the results of cyberbullying (both legal and psychological), and steps that can be taken to prevent it, each student outlines (**Handout 3**) and composes a draft of a letter to a preservice teacher [W.4, W.5]. A letter frame is provided for guidance (**Handout 4**). Each letter contains an introduction in which the student writes his/her name and age and tells briefly how he or she is connected with cyberbullying [W.2]. The letter also includes at least three startling facts from the articles that the student reads [W.7, W.8, W.9]. Usually, students choose to include more than three facts from their articles because they are so shocked by what they read. Finally, each letter must include advice to the preservice teacher regarding steps that he or she can take to help prevent cyberbullying.

Day 4

As is typical with the writing process, I ask students to revise and edit their drafts [W.4, W.5]. They conference with me and with at least two of their peers. During the conferences, I require that the students mark up their own letters. This helps to ensure that they are listening to their editors. Also, it helps the students maintain ownership of their work. I find that the students are much more invested in the revising and editing process for this writing piece than they are for typical research or class essays because they are writing for an authentic audience. They know that I will send these letters to graduate students at the local college who are pursuing a degree in education [W.4]. This is a big deal. The high school students want to present themselves as intelligent and well-informed individuals.

When I think about the benefits of implementing the cyberbullying letter-writing project in my class, two major points come to mind:

1. It answers the question "Why do we have to read this?" by connecting the themes of our reading with current social issues. It allows students to explore cyberbullying as it may concern their peers and even themselves. The issue may directly relate to adolescents who can identify with being bullied or taunted or ostracized.

 THEORY LINK (Bloom): Students *apply* their research to themselves and to preservice teachers.

2. It provides students with an authentic audience, therefore motivating them to polish their writing in a way that simply submitting to their teacher for a grade cannot.

 THEORY LINK (Dewey): Purposeful learning—students are not just earning a grade. Their work will inform future teachers.

Through the review of the cyberbullying articles, students hone their expository reading skills. They analyze and evaluate the information they read to choose the most pertinent facts to include in their letters. They synthesize this information into coherent letters written in a formal voice that reflects their awareness of audience. Each of these results is assessed through a grading checklist (**Handout 5**).

 THEORY LINK (Bloom): Students utilize a wide range of thinking skills during this experience.

This lesson enables students to respond to literature in a meaningful way. The combination of response to literary text and the use of informational text for the cyberbullying research make this lesson ideal for meeting the CCSS.

HANDOUT 1

MOOD AND TONE

1. Define the following:

Mood—_____

Tone—_____

2. Chart

Mood Cite two passages that indicate the mood of the work	Tone Cite two passages that indicate the tone of the work
Passage #1	Passage #1
Passage #2	Passage #2

3. How does the mood of the work compare with the tone of the work? What is the function of each?

HANDOUT 2

CYBERBULLYING—WEBSITES

www.stopcyberbullying.org/take_action/take_a_stand_against_cyberbullying.html

www.giveitaponder.com

www.athinline.org/

www.thatsnotcool.com

HANDOUT 3

CYBERBULLYING LETTER—ORGANIZER

Directions: Answer the following questions before you write your first draft of your cyberbullying letter.

1. What is the purpose of this letter?

2. How will you establish your expertise on this subject?

   (Have you been bullied/been a bully? Readings?)

3. Use the attached notes sheets to add research that supports your ideas.

Subtopic _____

Notes _____

_____

_____

_____

_____

_____

_____

(_____)

Author's last name or pg. #

Title of article

Subtopic _____

Notes _____

_____

_____

_____

_____

_____

_____

(_____)

Author's last name or pg. #

Title of article

HANDOUT 4

LETTER FRAME

Dear _____,

Introduction

State name, age, grade level, why you are writing this letter.

_____

_____

_____

Body paragraph(s)

State briefly how you are connected with cyberbullying.

_____

_____

_____

Include at least three startling facts from the articles that you read.

1. _____

_____

_____

2. _____

_____

_____

3. _____

_____

_____

Advice to the preservice teacher regarding steps that he or she can take to help prevent cyber-bullying.

_____

_____

_____

Body paragraph(s)

Wrap up by reminding reader of important facts, making a personal connection, and/or posing a question.

_____

_____

_____

Sincerely,
(Your Name)

HANDOUT 5

CYBERBULLYING LETTER—GRADING CHECKLIST

Content and Details (50 points) _____

- establishes a connection with reader
- informative
- accurate
- has many supporting details
- includes accurate citations
- logical
- interesting to read

45–50=excellent, 40–44=good, 35–39=fair, 33–34=poor, <33=failing

Organization (25 points) _____

- strong introduction that includes overview of details to be discussed
- strong topic sentences
- logical paragraph breakdown
- clear conclusion
- effective use of transitions
- overall fluency

23–25=excellent, 20–22=good, 17–19=fair, 15–16=poor, <15=failing

Mechanics and Readability (25 points) _____

- spelling
- punctuation
- grammar
- verb tense

23–25=excellent, 20–22=good, 17–19=fair, 15–16=poor, <15=failing

TOTAL_____

Lesson Plan Template

TOPIC:

This American Life (Grades 11–12)

CCSS STRAND:

Writing

TEXT TYPES AND PURPOSES:

Convey Experience

TIMING:

12 class periods

BACKWARD DESIGN COMPONENTS:

DESIRED RESULTS/CCSS ADDRESSED:

- Create a research-based script that tells the interviewee's story in a clear and coherent manner [W.3, W.4, W.7, W.8, W.9].

- Demonstrate understanding of effective storytelling devices modeled by *This American Life* by incorporating them into their Photo Stories [W.4, W.5].

- Publish the stories through Photo Story [W.6].

- Integrate information presented in diverse media [SL.2].

- Present stories appropriately through Photo Story [SL.4, SL.5].

ACCEPTABLE EVIDENCE:

- Interview notes pages
- Completed Photo Story

LEARNING EXPERIENCES AND INSTRUCTION:

- Day 1—Overview of *This American Life*; introduction to project.

- Day 2—Complete Pre-Interview Survey.

- Days 3–4—Compose expanded interview questions. Begin background research.

- Day 5—Expand interview.

- Days 6–7—Follow-up research.

- Days 8–11—Create Photo Stories.

- Day 12—Share with interviewees.

STRATEGIES:

- Modeling
- Cooperative Learning
- Writing Process

SUPPLEMENTAL RESOURCES:

- Historical website (www.history .com)

- *In Our Village*—this book is the story of a small village in Tanzania. This may provide an alternative option for organizing this project.

TECHNOLOGY/MEDIA OPPORTUNITIES:

- Inourvillage.org

- Student can also use iMovie to create their videos.

SERVICE LEARNING LINK:

- These videos could be aired at the local library.

- Videos might be aired at stores or banks that have televisions set up to distract people while they are waiting in line.

- Interviewees could "pay it forward" by recommending friends or family who might be strong interviewees for the future.

VARIATIONS:

- Develop a theme or focus for the project (e.g., veterans, immigrants, the anniversary of a local or national event).

- Connect with In Our Village—a program that encourages students to tell the stories of their neighborhoods (see Supplemental Resources and Technology/Media Opportunities).

- Ask interviewees about favorite books, and include excerpts from these books or have students research a book or poem that links with the interviewee's story and include passages in the presentation.

THIS AMERICAN LIFE

(Grades 11–12; Convey Experience)

Maureen Speaks

Ira Glass, the voice of *This American Life* radio broadcast, may be today's real-life version of Nick Carraway, a narrator who is clear, inviting, and just a bit judgmental while priding himself on not being so. *This American Life* can be heard on National Public Radio (NPR); podcasts are available at www.thisamericanlife.org; and the video version of the show is available on *Showtime*. Glass and his crew travel all over the country interviewing average people about everyday life. They record the interviews and edit them together with a perfect mix of narration, audio of the interviewees, sound effects, and music. The result is a collection of stories that revolve around a different theme each week. This may sound humdrum, but the thing is that once you really start talking and listening even to the seemingly average people in our midst, the ordinary becomes extraordinary.

Materials Needed

Podcasts of *This American Life*

Video of *This American Life*

Photo Story Download (www.microsoft.com/download/en/details.aspx?id=11132)

Paper and pens

Handouts

Timing

12 class periods (This may not be conducted on consecutive days)

Day 1—Overview of *This American Life;* introduce the project.

Day 2—Complete Pre-Interview Survey.

Days 3–4—Compose expanded interview questions. Begin background research.

Day 5—Expand interview.

Days 6–7—Follow-up research.

Days 8–11—Create Photo Stories.

Day 12—Share with interviewees.

TECH CONNECTION: Call a student up to be your "DJ" or producer for this.

Day 1

I have shared my love for this show with my students by teaming with my colleague, Nancy Regan, a social studies teacher, to develop our own *This American Life* Project. We listen with our students to a few episodes via free podcasts available on the NPR website. We also view a few stories that were aired on *Showtime.*

For both mediums, we discuss the effectiveness of the story-telling devices listed above (narration, audio of the interviewees, sound effects, and music).

Students quickly realize the importance of these devices in making the production a success [W.4, W.5, W.6].

 THEORY LINK (Gardner): Appeals to both Verbal-Linguistic and Visual-Spatial Intelligences (see below).

 TECH CONNECTION: Photo Story is an excellent tool for the classroom, and it is free!

Day 2

The next step in this process is to have students consider whom they would like to interview in order to make their own version of *This American Life.* They make this choice with the understanding that by participating in this experience, their teachers want them to develop a better understanding of a historical era and to know how to convey that understanding through Photo Story.

 DIFFERENTIATION TIP: Expectations may be adapted based on student ability.

Many students choose to interview a relative who has lived through an era that interests them. I have viewed *This American Life* projects based on veterans, the construction on New York City, and the experiences of a pastor and his wife at Woodstock. Once students choose their interviewees, they contact them for preliminary interviews (**Handout 1**) in which they confirm that there will be enough information on their chosen topic to create a good story [W.3]. They ask some basic questions and set up a convenient time for an in-person interview during which the students will record their interviewees' responses for playback on the Photo Story video that they will create [W.6].

Before the in-person interview, students conduct some research on the era or event that they will discuss with their interviewee [W7, W.8, W.9].

Days 3–4

After the preliminary interview, students continue their research and they develop more pointed interview questions.

Day 5

On the day of the expanded interview, the students must think on their feet and ask follow-up questions [SL.1].

 THEORY LINK (Gardner): Appeals to Interpersonal Intelligence.

THEORY LINK (Gardner): Students with strong Interpersonal Intelligence, Visual-Spatial Intelligence, and Musical-Rhythmic Intelligence will be strong leaders in this part of the process.

Also, they collect any pictures or documents that their interviewee thinks may be helpful in creating an impressive Photo Story.

Days 6–7

After the in-person interview, the students conduct even more research. Not only are they looking for more information on the time period or event, they may find songs or radio/video clips that relate to the stories that were shared. If needed, students may conduct yet another interview via phone or in person to fill in any gaps in their stories [W.5].

Days 8–11

The students create a script that they will read as their narration for their Photo Stories. They must include narration, clips of their interviewee's voice, and appropriate background music [SL.2, SL.5] (see **Handout 2** for scoring). Most students go far beyond this—including video and/or audio of famous speeches or newscasts from the events [SL.5]. The students work with me to edit their videos until they are pleased with their final products [W.5]. They create a pleasing cover for their DVDs and present their films to their interviewees at a breakfast screening [SL.4].

Day 12

At the breakfast screening, the pride that the students and their "stars" take in this project is so impressive. Students become invested in creating a high-quality product for the people they have chosen to cover. Also, often, the students are so well versed in technology that they find ways to make their Photo Stories better than I knew they could [W.6].

In addition to enhancing students' technology and media skills, this project focuses students on the elements of storytelling. They must consider the voice of the narrator. Is it biased? Is it appropriate for the audience? They must also

THEORY LINK (Bloom): Higher level thinking is required to compose follow-up questions.

THEORY LINK (Dewey): Point this out to students so they can see the *purpose* of this project for their own skills development.

consider if the clips of their interviewees' voices truly represent their characters. Finally, they must evaluate any effects (music, sound, photos, video, etc.) that they want to include [SL.2]. How do these enhancements affect their story? In developing the answer to this question, students are honing their analytical skills—the same question could be asked regarding the enhancements of literary devices such as simile or personification. I must note that the "on-the-spot thinking" that students must use in the interview portion of the preparation for this project enhances their ability to think at a higher level when under pressure.

HANDOUT 1

THIS AMERICAN LIFE—PRE-INTERVIEW SURVEY

This pre-interview survey is meant to prepare you and your interviewee for a more comprehensive interview. Your task is to pinpoint the era and events on which you would like to focus.

REMEMBER: Based on your findings, you will be conducting pre-interview **research**. You will have to create your interview questions and a timeline that reflects the era.

REMINDER!!!!!

Ask your interviewee to bring in photos or memorabilia from the era that you are covering.

SET AN INTERVIEW DATE!!!! _____

General Biographical Information:

What is your full name? _____

When were you born? _____

Where did you grow up? _____

How many people in your family? _____

Occupations (yours and/or your family members')?

Schooling?

Historical Background:

What era is most significant in your past?

When we sit down for the interview, what topics would you like to focus on? *What should we research?*

What active roles did you have?

What experiences do you remember most?

Add Your Own Questions:

Follow up on interesting facts/ideas/stories mentioned above.

1.

2.

3.

Good Interview Question Suggestions:

www.youthsource.ab.ca/teacher_resources/oral_question.html

REMINDER!!!!! Ask your interviewee to bring in photos or memorabilia from the era that you are covering.

SET AN INTERVIEW DATE!!!! _____

HANDOUT 2

THIS AMERICAN LIFE—RUBRIC

CATEGORY	4	3	2	1
Point of View— Purpose	Establishes a purpose early on and maintains a clear focus throughout.	Establishes a purpose early on and maintains focus for most of the presentation.	There are a few lapses in focus, but the purpose is fairly clear.	It is difficult to figure out the purpose of the presentation.
Voice— Consistency	Voice quality is clear and consistently audible throughout the presentation.	Voice quality is clear and consistently audible throughout the majority (85–95%) of the presentation.	Voice quality is clear and consistently audible through some (70–84%) of the presentation.	Voice quality needs more attention.
Soundtrack— Emotion	Music stirs a rich emotional response that matches the storyline well.	Music stirs a rich emotional response that somewhat matches the storyline.	Music is OK, and not distracting, but it does not add much to the story.	Music is distracting, inappropriate, or was not used.
Images	Images create a distinct atmosphere or tone that matches different parts of the story. The images may communicate symbolism and/ or metaphors.	Images create an atmosphere or tone that matches some parts of the story. The images may communicate symbolism and/or metaphors.	An attempt was made to use images to create an atmosphere/ tone but it needed more work. Image choice is logical.	Little or no attempt to use images to create an appropriate atmosphere/ tone.
Balance	The story purposefully and seamlessly incorporates factual information based on research and personal stories.	The story incorporates factual information based on research and personal stories, but is not as smooth or purposeful as a level 4 story.	The story seems to need more editing. It is either lacking factual information or personal information. It is disjointed and lacks balance.	The story needs extensive editing. It is disjointed and lacks balance.

(Continued)

(Continued)

CATEGORY	4	3	2	1
Rhetorical Devices	At least 5 rhetorical devices are used PROPERLY in the telling of the story. They are clearly highlighted on the typed copy of the narrative.	At least 4 rhetorical devices are used PROPERLY in the telling of the story. They are clearly highlighted on the typed copy of the narrative.	At least 3 rhetorical devices are used PROPERLY in the telling of the story. They are clearly highlighted on the typed copy of the narrative.	At least 2 rhetorical devices are used PROPERLY in the telling of the story. They are clearly highlighted on the typed copy of the narrative.

Part III

Speaking and Listening

6 The Benefits of CCSS for the Teaching of Speaking and Listening

I am a survivor of a concentration camp. My eyes saw what no person should witness: gas chambers built by learned engineers. Children poisoned by educated physicians. Infants killed by trained nurses. Women and babies shot by high school and college graduates. So, I am suspicious of education. My request is: Help your children become human. Your efforts must never produce learned monsters, skilled psychopaths or educated Eichmanns. Reading, writing, and arithmetic are important only if they serve to make our children more human.

—Dr. Haim Ginott, Holocaust survivor,
child psychologist, and author

We begin this chapter with the quote by Ginott because among the four strands of the Common Core State Standards (CCSS), Speaking and Listening, in our opinion, stand out as applied social skills. Through literature, we teach lessons about how to treat others. Through writing, we provide students with opportunities to reflect on their learning about how to treat others and to effect change in society. Language filters into each of the other three strands. The Speaking and Listening Anchor Standards are different because when students are developing the skills needed to meet these standards, in most cases, they are directly interacting with others. Thus, through learning attached to Speaking and Listening, students are able to put into practice cooperation, effective communication (this includes oral communication and the use of visual, digital, or quantitative support), strong listening skills, evaluative skills regarding a speaker, and awareness of audience. If students work with teachers to enhance these skills to the point of intrinsic knowing and understanding, it is reasonable to hope that they will not only be better prepared for college and the workplace, but that, as Dewey would approve, they will be better members of society.

In this chapter, we will introduce the CCSS for Speaking and Listening and provide commentary on the value of each of the Anchor Standards for increasing student college and career readiness. We hope that by teaching to these standards, teachers will be able to help students become the humane citizens called for by Ginott.

For easy reference, the Anchor Standards for Speaking and Listening that we will reference throughout this chapter are listed in Table 6.1. Shaded citations within the chapter come directly from these Anchor Standards. At the end of the chapter, we will go beyond the more general Anchor Standards and examine the 6–8, 9–10, and 11–12 grade-specific standards for "Presentation of Knowledge and Ideas."

COMPREHENSION AND COLLABORATION

In a study conducted by The Consortium (2006), which included the Partnership for 21st Century Skills of employers' perspectives of students' workforce readiness (regarding content knowledge and applied skills), Oral Communications, Teamwork/Collaboration, and Professionalism/Work Ethic

Table 6.1	Anchor Standards for Speaking and Listening (National Governors Association Center for Best Practices [NGA Center]/Council of Chief State School Officers [CCSSO], 2010b, p. 48)

Comprehension and Collaboration

1. Prepare for and participate effectively in a range of conversations and collaborations with diverse partners, building on others' ideas and expressing their own clearly and persuasively.

2. Integrate and evaluate information presented in diverse media and formats including visually, quantitatively, and orally.

3. Evaluate a speaker's point of view, reasoning, and use of evidence and rhetoric.

Presentation of Knowledge and Ideas

4. Present information, findings, and supporting evidence such that listeners can follow the line of reasoning and the organization, development, and style are appropriate to task, purpose, and audience.

5. Make strategic use of digital media and visual displays of data to express information and enhance understanding of presentations.

6. Adapt speech to a variety of contexts and communicative tasks, demonstrating command of formal English when indicated or appropriate.

Table 6.2	Rankings of Applied Skills by Employers (The Consortium, 2006, p. 20)

High School Grads	Two-Year College Grads	Four-Year College Grads
Applied Skill %	*Applied Skill %*	*Applied Skill %*
Professionalism/Work Ethic 80.3%	Professionalism /Work Ethic 83.4%	Oral Communications 95.4%
Teamwork/Collaboration 74.7%	Teamwork/Collaboration 82.7%	Teamwork/Collaboration 94.4%
Oral Communications 70.3%	Oral Communications 82.0%	Professionalism/Work Ethic 93.8%

were listed among the top three most important applied skills for high school, 2-year, and 4-year college graduates to have when entering the workplace (Table 6.2). Researchers defined Teamwork/Collaboration as the ability to "build collaborative relationships with colleagues and customers; be able to work with diverse teams, negotiate and manage conflicts" (The Consortium 2006, p. 15). Seventy-four percent of employers rated Teamwork/Collaboration as "very important" for high school graduates. Researchers defined Oral Communications as being able to "articulate thoughts, ideas clearly and effectively; have public speaking skills" (The Consortium, 2006, p. 15). Seventy percent of employers listed Oral Communications as "very important." Professionalism/Work Ethic rated first for employers of high school graduates (80.3%). The definition for Professionalism/Work Ethic in the study is the ability to "demonstrate personal accountability, effective work habits (e.g., punctuality, working productively with others, and time and workload management)" (The Consortium, 2006, p. 15).

Regardless of education level, these three applied skills ranked highest for employers; however, student ability to utilize these skills is deficient. Among the employers surveyed, 52.7% considered high school graduates entering the workforce deficient in Oral Communication skills; 34.6% considered them deficient in Teamwork/Collaboration; and 70.3% ranked them as deficient in Professionalism/Work Ethic (The Consortium, 2006, p. 32). Clearly, there is a need for us to help our students develop better interpersonal and social skills. The "Comprehension and Collaboration" Standards for Speaking and Listening help to address this need:

1. Prepare for and participate effectively in a range of conversations and collaboration with diverse partners, building on others' ideas and expressing their own clearly and persuasively.

2. Integrate and evaluate information presented in diverse media and formats including visually, quantitatively, and orally.

3. Evaluate speaker's point of view, reasoning, and use of evidence and rhetoric.

The first Standard is extremely important because it requires teachers to create lessons that encourage working with others. The Partnership for 21st Century Skills researchers asked surveyed employers to explain why they saw Professionalism/Work Ethic (which includes the ability to work with others) as important. Jim Kammerer, Director of Human Resources for a hospital in West Burlington, Iowa, explained how more and more he and his staff are doing behavioral interviewing during which they ask high school graduates questions like, "Describe how you worked together with classmates on a special project in high school. What role did you play? Did the team work well? What were the problems? What were the outcomes of the project?" (Partnership for 21st Century Skills, 2006, p. 23). Cheryl Forter, Human Resources Director for a manufacturer in Oklahoma, stated: "Just making good grades on a test doesn't necessarily make a good employee. It's the work ethic that makes the difference" (Partnership for 21st Century Skills, 2006, p. 23).

As teachers, we must create meaningful situations in which students communicate and collaborate effectively. Meyers (2010) writes, "Genuine dialogue rarely results in one privileged person gets to ask all of the questions while everyone else simply answers, deprived of the chance to articulate questions of their own" (p. 61). Burke (2010) comments on this imbalance:

> Kids often lack experience *using* questions to get information from people. They are more familiar with being peppered by questions from others: Where *were* you? Who were you *with?* What were you all *doing* there? Do you think these grades will get you into *college,* young man? You did *what?!* And so on. (p. 82)

The traditional teacher-directed classroom involves the teacher as the privileged person and the students as those who are unable to develop their own thinking. The disparity of power or privilege is reduced when students work in groups with their peers or when students are given the opportunity to lead the class. Vygotsky's (1978) concept of the zone of proximal development supports this idea. He described this zone as the difference between the level of development needed to solve a problem individually and the level needed to solve the problem through collaboration. This concept emphasizes the value of communication and collaboration.

Although Dewey would support the skills called for in Standard 1, Bloom would approve of Standards 2 and 3, which involve critical thinking such as *evaluate* information and a speaker's point of view and style, and *integrate (synthesize)* information gathered. In Chapter 3, we stated that students accept the Gettysburg Address and any other speech that has become famous as good writing. Standards 2 and 3 call for students to consider whether information is accurate, well-organized, or biased, and what elements make it this way. DeCosta, Clifton, and Roen (2010) address the evolution of literacy in today's classroom given the increased amount of information to which students are exposed because of technology: "Literacy involves social collaboration and interaction and a large skill and knowledge set that requires understanding, experiencing, and engaging collaboratively with many multimodal tasks in meaningful ways" (p. 17).

The CCSS note on Range and Content of Student Speaking and Listening summarizes the need for the standards concisely and clearly: "Whatever their intended major or profession, high school graduates will depend heavily on their ability to listen attentively to others so that they are able to build on others' meritorious ideas while expressing their own clearly and persuasively" (NGA Center/CCSSO, 2010, para. 1).

PRESENTATION OF KNOWLEDGE AND IDEAS

The need to assess students' presentation skills can be connected with the Partnership for 21st Century Skills survey mentioned earlier. Remember that 52.7% of employers stated that students were deficient in Oral Communication Skills—defined as the ability to "articulate thoughts, ideas clearly and effectively; have public speaking skills" (p. 15). Seventy percent of employers listed Oral Communications as "very important." Anchor Standards 4–6 for Speaking and Listening concern presentation skills:

> 4. Present information, findings, and supporting evidence such that listeners can follow the line of reasoning and the organization, development, and style are appropriate to task, purpose, and audience.
>
> 5. Make strategic use of digital media and visual displays of data to express information and enhance understanding of presentations.
>
> 6. Adapt speech to a variety of contexts and communicative tasks, demonstrating command of formal English when indicated or appropriate.

Most students are usually happy to work with others, as called for in Standards 1–3. Conversely, when asked to make presentations, many students become nervous or even panicked over the thought of standing in front of the room and stating what they have learned. Teaching to Standards 4–6 may give students the skills to help allay their anxiety. Standards 2 and 3 give students the ability to recognize common elements of strong public speaking. Common words can be found in Standard 3 and Standard 4 (evidence, reasoning, rhetoric/style). This emphasizes the bridge between the standards from analysis to application. Standard 5 correlates similarly with Standard 2—both concern digital media and visual displays as they support a presentation. Standard 6 addresses adapting language according to task.

It is ironic that in an age during which students are constantly communicating—in person, talking on their phones, texting, emailing, sharing videos via YouTube and Facebook—teachers need to address presentation skills. It seems that they are presenting all the time. Flynt and Brozo (2010) cite Felten on this paradox as it connects with visual literacy: "living in an image rich world . . . does not mean students naturally possess sophisticated visual literacy skills, just as continually listening to an iPod does not teach a person to critically analyze or create music" (p. 60). Students need our guidance to become polished presenters of knowledge. Just because they are doing it on their own does not mean that they are doing it well! That said, many of our students know more about technology than we do, so their visual or virtual displays may be far better than what we can envision. Flynt and Brozo (2010) discuss this: "When teachers incorporate podcasting or allow students to design eye-catching visual displays of their learning that can be used as artifacts of their learning, the teacher's role is akin to an orchestra conductor" (p. 527). We may not have the skills that students do with the "instruments" they are playing. However, we have the knowledge of style and organization to help students produce a masterpiece.

A CLOSER LOOK

When we examine the grade-specific standards for "Presentation of Knowledge and Ideas," the second set of Anchor Standards for "Speaking and Listening," we see the progression in sophistication that we have uncovered with the previous two sets of Anchor Standards for Reading and for Writing (Table 6.3).

Table 6.3 Speaking and Listening Standards for 6–8 (NGO Center/CCSSO, 2010b, p. 49)

Grade 6 Students	Grade 7 Students	Grade 8 Students
Presentation of Knowledge and Ideas	*Presentation of Knowledge and Ideas*	*Presentation of Knowledge and Ideas*
4. Present claims and findings, sequencing ideas logically and using pertinent descriptions, facts, and details to accentuate main ideas or themes; use appropriate eye contact, adequate volume, and clear pronunciation.	4. Present claims and findings, emphasizing salient points in a focused, coherent manner with pertinent descriptions, facts, details, and examples; use appropriate eye contact, adequate volume, and clear pronunciation.	4. Present claims and findings, emphasizing salient points in a focused, coherent manner with relevant evidence, sound valid reasoning, and well-chosen details; use appropriate eye contact, adequate volume, and clear pronunciation.
5. Include multimedia components (e.g., graphics, images, music, sound) and visual displays in presentations to clarify information.	5. Include multimedia components and visual displays in presentations to clarify claims and emphasize findings and salient points.	5. Integrate multimedia and visual displays into presentations to clarify information, strengthen claims and evidence, and add interest.
6. Adapt speech to a variety of contexts and tasks, demonstrating command of formal English when indicated or appropriate.	6. Adapt speech to a variety of contexts and tasks, demonstrating command of formal English when indicated or appropriate.	6. Adapt speech to a variety of contexts and tasks, demonstrating command of formal English when indicated or appropriate.

Table 6.4 Speaking and Listening Standards for 9–12 (NGO Center/CCSSO, 2010b, p. 50)

Grades 9–10 Students	Grades 11–12 Students
Presentation of Knowledge and Ideas	*Presentation of Knowledge and Ideas*
4. Present information, findings, and supporting evidence clearly, concisely, and logically such that listeners can follow the line of reasoning and the organization, development, substance, and style are appropriate to purpose, audience, and task.	4. Present information, findings, and supporting evidence conveying a clear and distinctive perspective, such that listeners can follow the line of reasoning, alternative or opposing perspectives are addressed, and the organization, development, substance, and style are appropriate to purpose, audience, and a range of formal and informal tasks.
5. Make strategic use of digital media (e.g., textual, graphical, audio, visual, and interactive elements) in presentations to enhance understanding of findings, reasoning, and evidence and to add interest.	5. Make strategic us of digital media (e.g., textual, graphical, audio, visual, and interactive elements) in presentations to enhance understanding of findings, reasoning, and evidence to add interest.
6. Adapt speech to a variety of contexts and tasks demonstrating command of formal English when indicated or appropriate.	6. Adapt speech to a variety of contexts and tasks demonstrating command of formal English when indicated or appropriate.

However, in this case, the focus is not only on the type of thinking that students must do, but also on the physical (e.g., eye contact, volume) and the social (e.g., the ability to make decisions based on an understanding of audience). Thus, these standards are a true meeting of the theories of Bloom and Gardner. Dewey would be pleased as well since the standards are leading students to be better able to function socially, and this would seem an important element in being a productive citizen.

When we look closely at Standard 4, we see that in Grades 6–8 there is a focus on content (main idea, description) and that the physical aspects of good presenting are made explicit (eye contact, volume, pronunciation). Grades 9–10 stress organization and introduce an awareness of the audience ("*listeners* can follow the line of reasoning," "organization, development, substance, and style are appropriate to purpose, *audience*, and task"). Grades 11–12 continue this consideration of audience and address "alternative or opposing perspectives."

For Standard 5, the use of multimedia becomes more pointed moving from simply including it to "clarify information" (Grade 6) to helping to make "salient points" (Grade 7) to adding interest (Grade 8) to becoming "strategic" and "interactive" in Grades 9–10 and 11–12. Standard 6 (which refers to language) remains the same in Grades 6–12.

CONCLUSION

In many ways, though speaking and listening are the most natural tasks for students (they began developing their speaking and listening skills long before they entered school), it is also the most challenging to teach. When we try to shift students from conversational chatter to more directed conversation or more formal presentations, this produces anxiety in them and a feeling of uncertainty for us as teachers because the assessment of speaking and listening skills feels nebulous at best. This is why the standards are so important for this domain.

Kipp-Newbold (2010) wrote of the difficulty she faced when trying to get her students to conduct insightful and meaningful conversations about literature. She wrote:

> I thought students who talk with their friends all the time, would naturally transfer those verbal skills to conversation about literature. But that was not the case. Student responses were hesitant and, despite my best efforts and intentions, conversations often became teacher-centered. (p. 74)

Students have become reliant on the traditional, teacher-centered classroom structure. They know that if they stay quiet, the teacher will be the speaker and they can choose whether or not they want to be listeners. In a setting in which the student takes on a more meaningful role as the teacher, as encouraged by the Speaking and Listening standards, the classroom dynamic shifts dramatically. That shift can be even more significant if consciously tied back to Haim Ginott's words at the start of this chapter. Let the development of our students as better communicators be even more purposeful by aligning our efforts with the concept of making them more humane.

When Maureen began requiring students to make a 10-minute oral presentation based on the analysis of a student-selected book, article, poem, or film clip, students moaned, and some parents even called to complain stating that students would rather hand in a written report. She explained to students and parents alike that the English standards for our state required students to develop their reading, writing, listening, and speaking skills. The speaking element felt comfortable for some of her students; however, even those who were confident in public speaking had difficulty adhering to a formal structure at times. Part of the reason for this was that students did not initially choose a topic that was intricate enough for analysis and discussion.

One of the first things that a student, Nick, in one of Maureen's classes presented was a clip from a movie in which a woman's chest was prominently featured. This was embarrassing for her, the cooperating teacher, and for some of his fellow students, and it yielded a failing grade for the presenter. Nick was correct in thinking that the clip would appeal to his audience because it was funny and a bit scandalous; however, he did not consider his entire audience, which included two teachers and some peers who found it inappropriate for the context in which he was presenting. What did he learn from the experience? He learned that he needed to better consider the materials he presented for class. What did Maureen learn? She learned that she needed to better screen the information that students present. She could not assume that students would know what was acceptable and what was not. Truly, Nick was always respectful in class but in this case his love for the movie clouded his vision regarding how suitable this clip was for the assignment and audience. The CCSS for Speaking and Listening (particularly the phrasing in SL.4 that refers to the presentation being "appropriate to task, purpose, and audience") would have helped Maureen to more effectively structure the parameters for this activity, leading Nick to more effectively measure his love for the movie against the appropriateness of the clip. Do you have students like Nick? If so, how do you help them succeed in speaking and listening? How do you help them become more humane? How can the CCSS help?

QUESTIONS/CHALLENGES/ PONDERING POINTS

1. How has the 21st century changed your perspective on teaching speaking and listening?

2. How complex are the speaking and listening tasks that you are assigning to your students?

3. In what ways do your students need to improve their speaking and listening skills?

4. How do you design curriculum that addresses your students' needs for improvement?

5. How do you modify instruction to promote the development of students' speaking and listening skills?

Speaking and Listening Lessons From the Classroom

7

INTRODUCTION

In this chapter, we will present three lessons that we believe are particularly effective for addressing the Common Core State Standards (CCSS) for Speaking and Listening. The Grades 6–8 lesson, Life in a Bag, provides a structure for students to make oral presentations based on a common class text (in this case, *The House on Mango Street*). The Grades 9–10 lesson, Editorial Videos, connects students with informational text and requires them to analyze visual media and digital displays such as video and photography. The Grades 11–12 lesson, Show and Tell, shifts the focus of the classroom from teacher-led discussion to student-led discussion by requiring students to develop interesting and context-appropriate presentations throughout the school year.

Life in a Bag is centered on students presenting their interpretations of characters and their personal connections to those characters by sharing objects that symbolize the characters and themselves. Editorial Videos involves students responding to the *New York Times* writer Nicholas Kristof's videos and developing their own campaign to address a global issue by utilizing some of the powerful elements of presentation and persuasion that they noted in the videos. Show and Tell allows students to select their own content for their presentations to the class. We call it Show and Tell, but don't let the seemingly elementary name fool you. This requires sophisticated planning and presentation skills, and when properly carried out, it prompts powerful class discussions.

As you read through these lessons and as you develop your own lessons, we encourage you to focus on how you can guide your students to meet the CCSS for Speaking and Listening that you examined in Chapter 6. Two sets of questions for reflection are listed below—specific questions pertaining to Speaking and Listening Anchor Standards and general questions regarding Lesson Design:

SPEAKING AND LISTENING ANCHOR STANDARDS REFLECTIVE QUESTIONS

How does the lesson require students to do one or more of the following?

1. Prepare and participate in a range of conversations and collaborations with diverse partners?

2. Build on others' ideas and express their own ideas clearly and persuasively?

3. Integrate and evaluate information presented in diverse media and formats?

4. Evaluate a speaker's point of view, reasoning, and use of evidence and rhetoric?

5. Present information, findings, and supporting evidence such that listeners can follow the line of reasoning?

6. Develop presentations in which the organization, development, and style are appropriate to task, purpose, and audience?

7. Make strategic use of digital media and visual displays?

8. Adapt speech to a variety of contexts and tasks demonstrating command of formal English language when indicated or appropriate?

LESSON DESIGN REFLECTIVE QUESTIONS

1. How does the lesson require close and multiple readings of grade-level complex text (classic, contemporary, or informational)?

2. How does my questioning require students to use the text as support for their interpretations/arguments?

3. How does the lesson incorporate varied thinking skills (e.g., read, summarize, analyze, interpret)? (Bloom)

4. How does the lesson include the three components of Backward Design: (a) desired results, (b) acceptable evidence, and (c) learning experiences?

5. How do I differentiate instruction, materials, and expectations for this particular lesson so that struggling students can be successful?

6. How does the lesson provide opportunities for technology/media use?

7. How does the lesson include research-based instructional strategies to promote effective teaching?

8. How can the lesson present opportunities for interdisciplinary connections?

9. How does the lesson provide opportunities for students with varied Multiple Intelligences to be successful? (Gardner)

10. How do I present the lesson in a way that encourages students to see the value of what they are learning (e.g., service learning, college- and career-readiness skills)? (Dewey)

Lesson Plan Template

TOPIC:

Life in a Bag (Grades 6–8)

CCSS STRAND:

Speaking and Listening

TEXT TYPES AND PURPOSES:

Convey Experience

TIMING:

2–3 class periods

BACKWARD DESIGN COMPONENTS:

DESIRED RESULTS/CCSS ADDRESSED:

- Participate in conversations about Life in a Bag, building on other's ideas and communicating one's own ideas clearly and persuasively [SL.1].

- Evaluate a speaker's point of view, reasoning, and use of evidence and rhetoric [SL.3].

- Present Life in a Bag in a way in which listeners can follow the line of reasoning [SL.4].

- Write comparison/contrast essay making effective use of content [W2].

ACCEPTABLE EVIDENCE:

- My Life in a Bag; My Character's Life in a Bag

- Presentations of Bags

- Comparison/Contrast Essay

LEARNING EXPERIENCES AND INSTRUCTION:

- Day 1—Prepare Paper Bags.

- Days 2–3—Present Paper Bags and begin essay writing.

STRATEGIES:

- Guidance and Monitoring

- Modeling

- Discussion

- Writing Process

SUPPLEMENTAL RESOURCES:

- Readers' Companion posted on Sandra Cisneros' website: http://sandracisneros.com/study_guides.php

TECHNOLOGY/MEDIA OPPORTUNITIES:

- Create a Photo Story of the Student's Life and Character's Life and compare and contrast in terms of culture.

SERVICE LEARNING LINK:

- Students present the activity to local senior citizens as an ice-breaker and then share favorite passages from the book with them.

- Students can engage in cross-cultural communication with classrooms in other countries via Skype or videoconferencing in which students in other countries share their Life in a Bag. Findings are displayed in the school lobby in order to increase peers' multicultural perspectives.

VARIATIONS:

- Use with other cultural texts (e.g., *Esperanza Rising* by Pam Muñoz Ryan; *In the Time of the Butterflies* [for the upper grades] by Julia Alvarez; *Dragonwings* by Laurence Yep).

- Use with movies and prepare Life in a Bag based on characters in films.

- Use with song lyrics that contain cultural themes.

LIFE IN A BAG

(Grades 6–8; Convey Experience)

Vicky Speaks

After a few days of reading and discussing *The House on Mango Street* (1991) by Sandra Cisneros, my students and I engage in postreading activities that are meant to promote cultural sensitivity. One such activity that could be used to achieve this goal is Life in a Bag, which requires students to think about their own cultural identity and how it relates to the cultural identity of a character in the story.

Materials Needed

Paper bags

Objects and/or index cards

Paper and pens

Handouts

Timing

2–3 class periods

Day 1—Prepare Paper Bags.

Days 2–3—Present Paper Bags and begin essay writing.

The Life in a Bag lesson is appropriate to teach with *The House on Mango Street* since the novel is centered on the coming-of-age experiences of Esperanza Cordero, an adolescent Chicana growing up in a poor neighborhood of Chicago and coming to terms with the influences of the Latino culture on her life. The novel consists of vignettes that paint pictures of Esperanza's neighborhood and its inhabitants (e.g., Rachel, Lucy, Sally), all colorful characters who are "stuck" in their situations, limited by their culture. Esperanza realizes that she needs to leave Mango Street in order to improve her life and to return someday to help the women on her block. In making text-to-self connections, students have a deeper, enduring understanding of the story. By exploring cultural aspects of themselves and other literary characters, students develop an understanding that culture informs our personalities, behaviors, ways of life, and essentially who we are.

This realization leads to student cross-cultural awareness and understanding. In terms of Speaking and Listening skills (reflected by the CCSS), I want my students to present the main cultural aspects of a character in a focused manner with evidence from the text [SL.4] as well as evaluate the reasoning and evidence of their classmates' character presentations [SL.3].

THEORY LINK (Bloom)
Students *comprehend* and *analyze* characters and make *applications* to self.

Day 1

For Life in a Bag, students prepare a small paper bag that contains six items that represent important aspects about their cultural identities (**Handout 1**). For those items that are too large to put in the bag, they can describe the item on an index card. After they are done with this activity, they prepare a bag for one of the main characters in the novel (of their choice). For example, I share with students that they may include a magnifying class in Esperanza's bag to symbolize how closely she examines life in her neighborhood. Because there may not be as many characters in *The House on Mango Street* as there are students, they can present on the same ones; however, the same characters should not be repeated multiple times, if possible. I poll students on which characters they would like to focus on and if the same ones are repeated several times, then I have students pick a character from a bag to ensure fairness.

Students brainstorm the contents that they plan to include in their bags and finish the bags at home where they will be able to find many of the items.

DIFFERENTIATION TIP: Students can present on a character of their choice.

Days 2–3

After all the bags are prepared, students practice presenting their descriptions of their bags' contents to a partner clearly and persuasively. I walk around to monitor students' work and guide them through the process of bag preparation and presentations.

THEORY LINK (Gardner): Appeals to Verbal-Linguistic Intelligence.

First students present their character's bag and then present their own to the whole class. After they present both bags, they talk about how they compare and contrast with the character they selected. I then ask them to take out any artifacts that would belong to both themselves as well as their character, and place them separately on the desk. This allows the students to visually assess how the students are similar to the character, which promotes the idea that despite our differences, we are all the same. We discuss our bags and how they represent ourselves and our characters and also evaluate the accuracy of the items in each bag [SL.1, SL.3]. All speakers are required to demonstrate effective communication skills including being organized, providing supporting evidence, speaking at an appropriate pace [SL.4], and so on (**Handout 2**). Classmates listening to the presentation are asked to take notes and evaluate it (**Handout 3**).

TECH CONNECTION: Students can create a Facebook account for their character on which they can also post Life in a Bag.

After everyone has presented, students are now ready to begin writing an essay in which they compare themselves with the character in the book [W.2] (**Handout 4**). The foundation of this essay is rooted in their own presentation and/or the notes that they took while listening to the presentations of their peers. They need to provide textual evidence to support the similarities and differences that they identify. This will be a less challenging assignment for them because they have completed all of the preparation for it. They have prepared and delivered oral presentations, received peer and teacher feedback, and listened and taken notes on their classmates' presentations. Students have the opportunity to revise any part of the Life in a Bag assignment based on received feedback; also, they may change their minds and write about different objects or different characters than the ones they presented.

DIFFERENTIATION TIP: Students can opt to write about different objects based on received input.

THEORY LINK (Dewey): Purposeful learning— Students develop global awareness.

THEORY LINK (Gardner): Appeals to Bodily-Kinesthetic and Interpersonal Intelligences.

Life in a Bag is an engaging and culturally responsive activity for several reasons: For one, students get the opportunity to talk about themselves and learn about each other. The culturally diverse students can share what it is like to live in the United States and how their native culture may conflict with mainstream culture. Students develop sensitivity toward peers whose experiences may be different from their own. Second, students learn about different cultures, the commonalities that they share, and have the opportunity to celebrate them. Third, they engage in a hands-on activity involving objects, which is always fun and enriching. Fourth, they have a chance to move around the room and interact with their peers, which can be exciting and appealing, especially to kinesthetic learners.

Through the Life in a Bag activity, students learn a lot about themselves, their classmates, their teacher, other diverse cultures, and spend some time getting to know their literary characters.

HANDOUT 1

MY LIFE IN A BAG

This diversity exercise uses cultural artifacts to help you clarify your cultural identity and build pride.

Directions: Bring six (6) items in a small paper bag that represent important cultural aspects about you as a person:

1. An award or object that feels to you like an award because you take great pride in possessing it.

2. An item that represents your *ethnic* identity (country or peoples you identify with) (e.g., food, dress).

3. A tradition, ritual, or celebration that defines your *cultural* identity (e.g., St. Patrick's Day parade).

4. A favorite book, poem, or song with which you can relate or that represents you.

5. One other object that symbolizes something important to you (e.g., a cross, a picture of your family).

6. One other object that symbolizes something important to you.

Be prepared to explain each item, why you selected it, and how it relates to you.

Based on Caruso, J. (1999). My life in a bag. *Electronic Magazine of Multicultural Education* [online], *1*(4). Retrieved from www .eastern.edu/publications/emme/1999fall/caruso.html.

MY CHARACTER'S LIFE IN A BAG

This diversity exercise uses cultural artifacts to help you "speak" for your character and clarify his or her cultural identity.

Directions: Select a main character in the novel *The House on Mango Street* by Sandra Cisneros. Bring six (6) items in a small paper bag that represent important cultural aspects about your character:

1. An award or an object that would feel like an award to your character.

   Provide evidence (1–2 quotations) from the novel.

2. An item that represents your character's *ethnic* identity (country or peoples he or she identifies with) (e.g., food, dress).

   Provide evidence (1–2 quotations) from the novel.

3. A tradition, ritual, or celebration that defines your character's *cultural* identity.

   Provide evidence (1–2 quotations) from the novel.

4. A favorite book, poem, or song that relates to your character or represents him or her.

   Provide evidence (1–2 quotations) from the novel.

5. An object that symbolizes something important to your character.

   Provide evidence (1–2 quotations) from the novel.

6. An object that symbolizes something important to your character.

   Provide evidence (1–2 quotations) from the novel.

   Be prepared to explain each item, why you selected it, and how it relates to your character.

Based on Caruso, J. (1999). My life in a bag. *Electronic Magazine of Multicultural Education* [online], *1*(4), 2 paragraphs. Retrieved from www.eastern.edu/publications/emme/1999fall/caruso.html.

HANDOUT 2

LIFE IN A BAG—ORAL PRESENTATION RUBRIC

CATEGORY	4	3	2	1
Cultural Aspects of Character	Shows a full understanding of the cultural aspects of the character.	Shows a good understanding of the cultural aspects of the character.	Shows a partial understanding of the cultural aspects of the character.	Does not seem to understand the character very well.
Cultural Aspects of Self	Shows a full understanding of the cultural aspects of self.	Shows a good understanding of the cultural aspects of self.	Shows a partial understanding of the cultural aspects of self.	Does not seem to understand the cultural aspects of self very well.
Items in Bag	Each bag contains 6 items.	Each bag contains 5 items.	Each bag contains 4 items.	Each bag contains fewer than 3 items.
Development of Supporting Evidence	Provides supporting evidence clearly and fully.	Satisfactorily provides supporting evidence.	Partially provides supporting evidence.	Minimally provides supporting evidence.
Organization and Coherence	Exhibits an exemplary logical and coherent structure.	Exhibits satisfactorily a logical and coherent structure.	Partial coherence and cohesiveness.	Minimal coherence and cohesiveness.
Stays on Topic	Stays on topic all (100%) of the time.	Stays on topic most (90–99%) of the time.	Stays on topic some (75%–89%) of the time.	It was hard to tell what the topic was.
Uses Complete Sentences	Always (99–100%) speaks in complete sentences.	Mostly (80–98%) speaks in complete sentences.	Sometimes (70–79%) speaks in complete sentences.	Rarely speaks in complete sentences.

(Continued)

(Continued)

CATEGORY	4	3	2	1
Posture and Eye Contact	Stands up straight, looks relaxed and confident. Establishes eye contact with everyone in the room during the presentation.	Stands up straight and establishes eye contact with everyone in the room during the presentation.	Sometimes stands up straight and establishes eye contact.	Slouches and/or does not look at people during the presentation.
Speaks Clearly	Speaks clearly and distinctly all (100%) the time.	Speaks clearly and distinctly almost all (95%–99%) the time.	Speaks clearly and distinctly most (94–85%) of the time.	Often mumbles or cannot be understood.
Preparedness	Student is completely prepared and has obviously rehearsed.	Student seems pretty prepared but might have needed a couple more rehearsals.	The student is somewhat prepared, but it is clear that rehearsal was lacking.	Student does not seem at all prepared to present.
Comprehension	Student is able to accurately answer almost all questions posed by classmates about the topic.	Student is able to accurately answer most questions posed by classmates about the topic.	Student is able to accurately answer a few questions posed by classmates about the topic.	Student is unable to accurately answer questions posed by classmates about the topic.
Listens to Other Presentations	Listens intently. Does not make distracting noises or movements.	Listens intently but has one distracting noise or movement.	Sometimes does not appear to be listening but is not distracting.	Sometimes does not appear to be listening and has distracting noises or movements.
Evaluates Peers	Answers all three evaluation questions when evaluating each peer.	Answers two evaluation questions when evaluating each peer.	Answers one evaluation question when evaluating each peer.	Answers no evaluation questions when evaluating each peer.

HANDOUT 3

PEER EVALUATION QUESTIONS

1. Discuss one thing that you liked about the presentation.

2. Discuss one thing that showed effort.

3. Discuss one thing that could be improved.

HANDOUT 4

COMPARISON/CONTRAST ESSAY

In this essay, you are to compare and contrast the cultural aspects of yourself with those of a character in *The House on Mango Street* by Sandra Cisneros. Follow the outline below:

Paragraph 1: Introduction: State the purpose of your essay. Include the title and author of the book.

Paragraph 2: Describe THREE cultural aspects of yourself.

1. _____

2. _____

3. _____

Paragraph 3: Describe THREE cultural aspects of your character. Provide textual evidence.

1. _____

2. _____

3. _____

Paragraph 4: Discuss the similarities and differences.

Similarities:

_____

_____

Differences:

_____

_____

Paragraph 5: Conclusion: Summarize main ideas. End with style. For instance, include a rhetorical question or a quote.

Lesson Plan Template

TOPIC:
Editorial Videos (Grades 9–10)

CCSS STRAND:
Speaking and Listening

TEXT TYPES AND PURPOSES:
Argue/Persuade

TIMING:
2 class periods

BACKWARD DESIGN COMPONENTS:

DESIRED RESULTS/CCSS ADDRESSED:

- Analyze and discuss the content and style of Kristof's videos [SL.1, SL.2, SL.3].
- Research an issue of concern [R.7, W.7, W.8, W.9, SL.2].
- Deliver an effective, well-organized, and logical presentation (including visual aids and media) on an issue that matters to them (e.g., cell phones) [SL.4, SL.5, SL.6].

ACCEPTABLE EVIDENCE:

- Completed video response organizer
- Logical and effective campaign presentation

LEARNING EXPERIENCES AND INSTRUCTION:

- Day 1—View Kristof's videos and respond.
- Days 2–3—Research and develop a campaign based on a social concern.
- Day 4—Present speech.

STRATEGIES:

- Discussion
- Cooperative learning

SUPPLEMENTAL RESOURCES:

- *The New York Times*
- Ted Talks (www.ted.com)
- YouTube.com

TECHNOLOGY/MEDIA OPPORTUNITES:

- Students may create their own videos or songs for Show and Tell (see following lesson plan).

SERVICE LEARNING LINK:

- Students focus on social issues and become advocates for a cause.
- Students may consider varied voices/points of view on an issue and present those voices to their peers. This may lead to other campaigns.

VARIATIONS:

- Allow students who are unable to attend parent night or who are not comfortable speaking publicly to create campaign posters. Discuss how to incorporate Kristof's powerful elements into visual displays.
- Contrast opposing viewpoints on an issue.

EDITORIAL VIDEOS

(Grades 9–10; Argue/Persuade)

Vicky and Maureen Speak

Nicholas Kristof, an editorial writer for the *New York Times*, writes about powerful topics of local and global importance. Kristof, like many journalists today, recognizes that people are accessing their news in different ways. Therefore, he has created a blog (http://kristof.blogs.nytimes.com/) that includes several videos of his travels and his interactions with people from around the globe. In this lesson, students watch Kristof's videos and use them as a springboard to write speeches with a call for action that they present at a school event.

Materials Needed

Access to Nicholas Kristof's online videos

Projector and screen

Paper and pens

Handouts

Timing

4 class periods

Day 1—View Kristof's videos and respond.

Days 2–3—Research and develop a campaign based on a social concern.

Day 4—Present speech.

Day 1

Many students are introduced to important social issues by watching Kristof's videos. To aide their comprehension and analysis, they complete a handout with some of their notes about important details, powerful reactions, questions for further exploration, and reflection on how taking in information via video compares with reading it (**Handout 1**) [SL.1, SL.2, SL.3].

 THEORY LINK (Gardner): Appeals to Verbal-Linguistic, Intrapersonal, and/or Visual-Spatial Intelligences.

Some of the most powerful videos for students are Kristof's reports from The Democratic Republic of Congo. Kristof shows the victims of incredibly brutal acts that result from a country torn apart by violence and greed. Much of the war in the Congo comes from the minerals that are purchased to make cell phones and laptops. It is important to prescreen Kristof's videos because some may be too graphic for some students; however, the wide variety of videos that he posts will allow for ample choices.

Days 2–3

Viewing Kristof's video makes students want to take some kind of action. After watching the videos, students are asked to get into groups and research an issue of concern that they will present to parents, teachers, and administrators by setting up an information table in the lobby at an upcoming school event such as Parent Night, a school concert, or a sporting event (**Handout 2**). Students conduct research by viewing more videos and reading articles on the topic that concerns them. They then formulate a presentation that con-

sists of information to raise awareness and three solid reasons that a certain action needs to take place. The call for action can include asking the audience to write letters or make phone calls to politicians, to contribute money, or to sign a petition. An example of the latter can be requesting parents, teachers, and administrators to sign an online petition calling for major companies to eliminate the use of conflict minerals in their products [SL.4, SL.6].

THEORY LINK (Gardner): Appeals to Logical-Mathematical Intelligence.

THEORY LINK (Dewey): Purposeful learning—students are conducting research and utilizing their speaking and listening skills for the greater good.

In addition to writing a speech, students consider what visual aids may be effective in getting adults to take action. For example, they may opt to show parts of the videos that they have viewed or create posters with striking images and startling statistics.

They may also consider ways to expand the reach of their presentation beyond the event by providing "take-away" materials such as pamphlets with key details or stickers with a slogan and a link to a website with more information [SL.5].

THEORY LINK (Gardner): Appeals to Verbal-Linguistic Intelligence and/or Interpersonal Intelligence.

In order to prepare for this, students must use their tech literacy to navigate through sites (e.g., www.enoughproject.org) that offer an action to address their issue of concern [R.7, W.7, W.8, W.9, SL.2]. After they draft their presentation, students assign parts of the speech to each group member so that every student has a speaking part.

THEORY LINK (Gardner): Appeals to Logical/Mathematical Intelligence.

Students develop their speaking and listening skills during the research part of the project as they watch the videos and assess which websites to use and what information to include in their speeches.

THEORY LINK (Gardner): Appeals to Interpersonal Intelligence.

Day 4

This lesson culminates with students' presenting at a school event. Students hone their speaking and listening skills during their presentations when they will need to call people to action and be able to think on their feet as they answer questions from the audience.

Kristof is a great "go-to guy" for examining an issue; however, we all have favorite columnists who may be posting videos. It is important to consider varying the viewpoints of the journalists that we "invite" into our classrooms [SL.3]. Regardless of the journalists the teacher chooses to follow, if the content is significant to students, then with note-taking guidelines and encouragement regarding a follow-up action plan, these videos can spark students' most meaningful work.

HANDOUT 1

VIEWING REFLECTION

Important Details

      * _____

      * _____

      * _____

Powerful Reactions

      ! _____

      ! _____

Questions for Further Exploration

      ? _____

      ? _____

REFLECTION

How does viewing this information compare with reading information on the same topic?

HANDOUT 2

SCHOOL EVENT FOR YOUR GLOBAL ISSUE CAMPAIGN

OVERVIEW

For the next few days, you will be working with your fellow students to change your world. Based on one of the issues that stands out to you after watching several of Nicholas Kristof's videos, you will design a campaign to call people to take action. You will present your campaign at an upcoming school event, and you will be graded based on the grading checklist below along with Listener Feedback Forms that will be placed at your information table.

STEP 1: Research

Once your group has agreed upon an issue of concern, gather information from at least two sources (such as www.enough.org; www.IRC.org; or www.amnesty.org). See the attached research note-taking sheets.

STEP 2: Formulate Your Campaign

- Outline your speech (see attached sheet)
- Agree upon visual displays

  o Will you show videos?
  o Have you designed posters to draw attention to your table?
  o Will people take away a physical reminder (pamphlet, flyer, campaign sticker)?

- Assign apeaking roles

  o Speaker #1 is assigned . . .
  o Speaker #2 is assigned . . .
  o Speaker #3 is assigned . . .
  o Speaker #4 is assigned . . .

- Assign additional table roles

  o Who will keep track of the number of people who listen to your speech?
  o Who will keep track of the number of people who take action based on your speech?
  o Who will ensure that table visitors complete feedback forms and drop them in the feedback envelope?
  o Who will hand out and explain the take-away information so that people don't just put it in their pockets and forget about it? This person must be able to briefly point out impressive, short segments of information on each handout.

STEP 3: Present at a School Event

This is about more than just earning a grade. This is about changing your world!

NOTE-TAKING GUIDE I

Issue of Concern: _____

Source #1: _____

BACKGROUND

Where is the injustice happening?

How long has this been going on?

Who is involved?

(Who are the "bullies"? Who are the victims?)

Why is the injustice happening?

What are some of the effects of this injustice?

(on families, living conditions, safety, health, income, etc.)

ACTION

What organizations are working to address this problem? How are they addressing it?

What can we do to help?

POWERFUL STATISTICS/QUOTES TO HIGHLIGHT ON CAMPAIGN VISUALS

1.

2.

NOTE-TAKING GUIDE II

Issue of Concern: _____

Source #2: _____

BACKGROUND

Where is the injustice happening?

How long has this been going on?

Who is involved?

(Who are the "bullies"? Who are the victims?)

Why is the injustice happening?

What are some of the effects of this injustice?

(on families, living conditions, safety, health, income, etc.)

ACTION

What organizations are working to address this problem? How are they addressing it?

What can we do to help?

POWERFUL STATISTICS/QUOTES TO HIGHLIGHT ON CAMPAIGN VISUALS

1.

2.

SPEECH OUTLINE

I. Introduction: State the basic facts.

   A. Who is being hurt?

   B. What is happening to them?

   C. Why is it happening?

   D. Where is this happening?

   E. When did this begin?

II. Provide more details to develop your reasoning (use your note-taking guide!).

   A. State more statistics.

   B. Include an anecdote (this may be where you refer to a video).

III. Introduce the agency that you believe can effect the greatest change regarding this issue.

   A. What has this agency done?

   B. Why do you consider it trustworthy?

   C. What is the agency currently doing to address this issue?

IV. Call for Action: What do you want the audience to do? Explain.

V. Conclusion: End with a summary, clincher, an inspiring quote, fact, and so on.

LISTENER FEEDBACK FORM

Reviewer's name: _____

Students who presented to you: _____

Topic of presentation: _____

Please note any new information or striking statistics/anecdotes that students shared with you.

In addition to conveying the main ideas of the global issue that concerns them, did students provide you with information regarding simple steps that you can take to invoke change? Please explain.

1. How clear was the students' presentation of the information?

Very clear   Somewhat clear   Somewhat unclear   Unclear

2. How well did students convey their passion or concern for this topic?

Very well   Somewhat well   Somewhat poorly   Poorly

3. Other comments?

THANK YOU FOR YOUR TIME!

CAMPAIGN GRADING CHECKLIST

Research Notes Sheets (20 Points) _____

- Clear and informative notes regarding background
- Clear and informative notes regarding action
- Clear and informative notes regarding statistics/quotes

18–20=excellent, 16–17=good, 14–15=fair, 12–13=poor, <12=failing

Speech Outline (40 Points) _____

- All components (Roman numerals, letters) are addressed
- Represents a fluid speech
- Fairly divided among group members

36–40=excellent, 32–35=good, 28–31=fair, 24–27=poor, <24=failing

Visual Displays (20 Points) _____

- Videos are appropriate for the event and show pertinent information related to the global issue.
- Posters are visually effective (photos, artwork, slogan, statistics).
- Take-away is accurate, informative, and concise.

18–20=excellent, 16–17=good, 14–15=fair, 12–13=poor, <12=failing

Listener Feedback (10 points) _____

- Listeners noted new/pertinent information.
- Statistics and anecdotes were striking enough to provoke action.
- Effective communication (clearly conveyed information)
- Effective communication of passion or concern for the cause

9–10=excellent, 8=good, 7=fair, 6=poor, <6=failing

Use of Class Time (10 points) _____

9–10=excellent, 8=good, 7=fair, 6=poor, <6=failing

TOTAL _____

Lesson Plan Template

TOPIC:
Show and Tell (Grades 11–12)

PURPOSE/TYPE OF WRITING:
Explain/Inform

CCSS STRAND:
Speaking and Listening

TIMING:
1 class period

BACKWARD DESIGN COMPONENTS:

DESIRED RESULTS/CCSS ADDRESSED:

- Prepare an analysis of the content, style, and point of view of an author as represented in a book, poem, song lyrics, or television/movie script [R4, R5, SL.1, SL.2, SL.3, L3, L5].
- Deliver an effective, well-organized, and logical presentation that incorporates technology through the use of the LCD projector [SL.4, SL.5].
- Use appropriate formal voice and posture for their presentations [SL.6].

ACCEPTABLE EVIDENCE:

- Completed presentation organizer
- Logical and effective presentation

LEARNING EXPERIENCES AND INSTRUCTION:

- Day 1—Students give a 10–15-minute presentation on a brief passage from a self-selected source.

STRATEGIES:

- Modeling
- Discussion

SUPPLEMENTAL RESOURCES:

- *New York Times*
- Ted Talks (www.ted.com)
- IMDB movie summaries
- Lyrics.com

TECHNOLOGY/MEDIA OPPORTUNITIES:

- Students may create their own videos or songs for Show and Tell.

SERVICE LEARNING LINK:

- Students focus on social issues and become advocates for a cause.
- They may research community organizations that are addressing a social issue and coordinate a class effort to help create change.

VARIATIONS:

- Allow students to present in pairs or small groups.
- Create a theme for each month. All presentations must relate to said theme.

SHOW AND TELL

(Grades 11–12; Explain/Inform)

Maureen Speaks

Remember when you were young, and your teacher told you it was your turn to present for Show and Tell? You brought in your prized possessions, a new toy, a special picture . . . once my mom brought in our new kittens (how cool!). Why can't we maintain that spirit of sharing and excitement in the high school classroom? Each Friday, my students and I attempt to do just that by participating in a literary version of Show and Tell.

Materials Needed

Student's choice of text (book, poem, news article, movie scene or song)

LCD projector

Paper and pens

Handouts

Timing

1 class period (for three presenters)

Day 1—Students give a 10–15 minute presentation on a brief passage from a self-selected source.

THEORY LINK (Gardner): Appeals to all types of Intelligences.

Day 1

Believe it or not, this assignment creates anxiety for many of my students. Like many, they fear public speaking as much as death! The good news is that since all students must present eventually, they tend to be a supportive audience. They behave in the way that they hope their peers will when they are at the podium. Thus, this assignment provides a very low-pressure environment in which students can develop their formal speaking skills. Regardless of what the students choose to present, they must submit an electronic copy of the text for approval by the day before their presentations. They highlight their documents according to the questions answered on their presentation organizers (**Handout 1**).

DIFFERENTIATION TIP: Students choose works written at a level with which they can be successful.

DIFFERENTIATION TIP: This can easily be modified for struggling learners to include only one significant passage, one literary element, and two discussion questions.

Students must address the following:

1. Why did you choose this work?

2. Where did you first discover this work?

3. Discuss the effect the passage has on you.

4. What is the theme of the work? [R.2]

5. Discuss the effect of two literary elements used by the author. [R.4, SL.3, L.3, L.5]

6. Compose four open-ended discussion questions for your peers. [SL.1]

THEORY LINK (Bloom): When I introduce this assignment, I spend time discussing the value of open-ended questions. With this in mind, students compose questions that call for varied types of thinking.

THEORY LINK (Gardner): This is a great opportunity for success for students who may struggle with expressing their ideas in writing, but who have strong interpersonal skills.

TECH CONNECTION: Many students must adapt to facing their audience while navigating information on a screen. Again, it is good for them to develop skills in this area in a supportive, low-pressure environment.

In addition to their written preparation, I tell students that they need to rehearse their presentations [SL.1, SL.6]. Inevitably, there are those students who must experience stage fright in front of their peers in order to appreciate the importance of this step in the process of presenting. Of course, there are those who are born performers and teachers as well. The difference is clear very quickly!

On the day of Show and Tell, students project their documents using the LCD projector, introduce the topic, read the passage (or call on volunteers to help with reading), discuss highlighted passages and literary elements, and conduct a discussion based on the questions they developed [SL.5]. They are graded on their preparation, awareness of content, formal voice, presentation skills, and discussion questions (**Handout 2**). The "audience" is graded based on their listening skills as shown through their ability to answer the discussion questions. Also, audience members are given the opportunity to ask questions of their own. The presenter's ability to respond reflects his or her level of preparation [SL.1].

Show and Tell evokes fear, excitement, and my favorite response—revelation. I cannot tell you how many times students have chosen to present song lyrics and suddenly in preparing with me after school said, "I never really knew what this was about until now." Often while presenting to their peers, the same response is heard. Another favorite result of a strong presentation is a heated debate. This usually occurs when students present articles on "hot topics" such as drug testing, drinking age, driving age, cell phone use in schools, and Facebook. In the unlikely event that students' presentations are completed early, I have a few controversial articles ready to put up on my LCD projector for reading and discussion. Time for my own Show and Tell is rare (it most often happens that I present due to a student presenter's absence). Students are eager to keep the time afforded to them. This means interesting topics [SL.1], skillful analysis [R.4, SL.3, L.3, L.5], and provoking discussion questions [SL.1].

This exercise serves several purposes: It allows students to become teachers for 10–15 minutes. They must think about what topics matter to them and what writing has had an effect on them. They must also consider if this topic/writing will be interesting to their peers.

They must have a strong level of comprehension of the piece they have chosen. Also, they must analyze and interpret the author's choices regarding literary elements. In addition, their questioning often involves application to their own experiences. Finally, this provides students with an opportunity to hone their speaking and presentation skills.

Another benefit of Show and Tell is that students get to feel what it is like to be a teacher. Yes, we love what we do, but we do face certain challenges in planning, presenting, and encouraging participation. Having students take a few minutes in our shoes can help them empathize with us both in our successes and our frustrations. If students can empathize with their teachers, they may be better able to cooperate and create the most productive work environment possible.

THEORY LINK (Gardner): Appeals to Interpersonal Intelligence.

THEORY LINK (Dewey): Purposeful learning—students must consider what matters to them and to their audience.

THEORY LINK (Bloom): Students exhibit a progression from *comprehension* to *analysis*, *evaluation*, and *application* to self and society.

THEORY LINK (Dewey): Purposeful learning—students understand that these are important skills for job interviews and in creating confidence discussing information at a college level.

HANDOUT 1

SHOW AND TELL—PREPARATION GUIDE

Directions: Complete this entire organizer before presenting. This will serve as your outline when you are standing at the podium.

Introduction

How did you find this work?

_____

_____

_____

Why did you choose this work? What do you like about it? What do you find interesting?

_____

_____

_____

Passages

List 2 significant passages for discussion:

Passage 1:

_____

_____

Why I like it:

_____

_____

Passage 2:

_____

_____

Why I like it:

_____

_____

Theme

Based on your analysis of the work, state the theme:

_____

_____

Literary Elements

Identify 2 literary elements in your piece and their effects on the reader/viewer:

Possible choices include but are not limited to symbolism, conflict, significant setting, characterization, irony, dramatic irony, juxtaposition, metaphor, simile, alliteration.

Literary Element 1:

_____

_____

Effect:

_____

_____

Literary Element 2:

_____

_____

Effect:

_____

_____

Discussion Questions

Based on the above, compose 4 class discussion questions:

1. _____

2. _____

3. _____

4. _____

HANDOUT 2

SHOW AND TELL—RUBRIC

Category	4	3	2	1
Preparedness	Student is completely prepared and has obviously rehearsed.	Student seems pretty prepared but might have needed a couple more rehearsals.	The student is somewhat prepared, but it is clear that rehearsal was lacking.	Student does not seem at all prepared to present.
Content	Shows a full understanding of the content. Insightful analysis.	Shows a good understanding of the content. Good analysis.	Shows a good understanding of parts of the content. Basic analysis.	Does not seem to understand the content very well. No analysis.
Introduction	Clearly states how the piece was found. Strong case for connection to others/class content.	Somewhat clearly states how the piece was found. Good case for connection to others/class content.	Mentions how the piece was found. Fair case for connection to others/class content.	Fails to state how the piece was found. No case for connection to others/class content.
Formal Voice	Impressive and appropriate word choice.	Good word choice.	Informal word choice.	Informal. Too many "ums" and "likes."
Enthusiasm	Facial expressions and body language generate a strong interest and enthusiasm about the topic in others.	Facial expressions and body language sometimes generate a strong interest and enthusiasm about the topic in others.	Facial expressions and body language are used to try to generate enthusiasm, but seem somewhat unnatural.	Very little use of facial expressions or body language. Did not generate much interest in topic being presented.

Category	4	3	2	1
Questioning	Open-ended questions that encourage meaningful discussion. Follow-up questions reflect excellent listening skills.	Some open-ended discussion questions and follow-up questions.	Mostly yes/no questions. Unable to spark discussion.	Student does not have the minimum number of discussion questions. Little or no follow-up questions.
Comprehension	Student is able to accurately answer all questions posed by classmates/ teacher about the topic.	Student is able to accurately answer most questions posed by classmates/ teacher about the topic.	Student is able to accurately answer a few questions posed by classmates/ teacher about the topic.	Student is unable to accurately answer questions posed by classmates/ teacher about the topic.

Part IV

Language

8 The Benefits of CCSS for the Teaching of Language

Grammar, perfectly understood, enables us not only to express our meaning fully and clearly, but so to express it as to enable us to defy the ingenuity of man to give to our words any other meaning than that which we ourselves intend them to express.

—*William Cobbett*

Vicky will never forget the time she was in a watch repair store in her parents' native country, Greece, picking up her watch. She must have been 12 at the time and despite the fact that her Greek was near nativelike, she made occasional errors. When the repairman gave the watch back to her, she was excited that it was repaired and innocently asked, "And so is it *supposedly* fixed now?" What she really wanted to ask was, "And so is it *actually* fixed now?" The repairman looked at her angrily and furiously exclaimed: "What do you mean, Miss? Are you implying that I am lying to you and that I didn't fix your watch?" She looked at him puzzled, and after realizing her mistake, apologized and bid him farewell. Using the right words to communicate the exact meaning intended is a difficult task in any language. Knowing when and how to say what to whom—known as the conventions of grammar (spoken and written) (Rothstein & Rothstein, 2009)—requires an understanding of the rules of grammar as well as the context of language use, which includes the culture in which it is embedded. Vicky's example shows that culture shapes intended meaning. Her experience emphasizes the difficulty of what Cobbett refers to as being able "to express our meaning fully and clearly."

Teaching students to develop knowledge of vocabulary and language conventions in the classroom is also not an easy task. There are a few words that Maureen would like to ban from her classroom such as "retard" or "gay" (as used in a derogatory sense) or phrases such as "I don't know" or "I can't" (when students have not taken a moment to struggle or try). These choices probably will not surprise you, but the next few may—"nice," "good," "interesting." These words are too bland and too easy to lean on. Some of us would admit to our own intellectual laziness when it comes to these words. It is easy to tell students that their comments or responses were "nice," "good," or "interesting," but as teachers, we need to make a conscious effort to individualize our responses since we would like to see the same thing happen with our students. For instance, why is a character nice or good? What actions support that description? After considering those actions, is there a more apt word to use to describe said character (e.g., "generous," "empathetic," "selfless")? Also, we would hope that many of the works that we read in class are interesting. What makes each work interesting? Again, is there a better descriptor ("inspiring," "insightful," "emblematic of a much needed new perspective")?

The Common Core State Standards (CCSS) for Language require students to develop their understanding and command of vocabulary and general language conventions and to apply their knowledge to analyze others' style of speaking and writing and make choices about their own. In this chapter, we will introduce the CCSS for Language and provide commentary on the value of each of the Anchor Standards for increasing student college and career readiness. We hope that by teaching to these standards, teachers will be able to help students improve the form of their writing and speaking. For easy reference, the Anchor Standards for Language that we will reference throughout this chapter are listed in Table 8.1. At the end of the chapter, we will go beyond the more

Table 8.1	Anchor Standards for Language (National Governors Association Center for Best Practices [NGA Center]/Council of Chief State School Officers [CCSSO], 2010b, p. 51)

LANGUAGE

Conventions of Standard English

1. Demonstrate command of the conventions of standard English grammar and usage when writing or speaking.

2. Demonstrate command of the conventions of standard English capitalization, punctuation, and spelling when writing.

Knowledge of Language

3. Apply knowledge of language to understand how language functions in different contexts, to make effective choices for meaning or style, and to comprehend more fully when reading or listening.

Vocabulary Acquisition and Use

4. Determine or clarify the meaning of unknown and multiple-meaning words and phrases by using context clues, analyzing meaningful word parts, and consulting general and specialized reference materials, as appropriate.

5. Demonstrate understanding of word relationships and nuances in word meanings.

6. Acquire and use accurately a range of general academic and domain-specific words and phrases sufficient for reading, writing, speaking, and listening at the college and career readiness level; demonstrate independence in gathering vocabulary knowledge when considering a word or phrase important to comprehension or expression.

general Anchor Standards and examine the 6–8, 9–10, and 11–12 grade-specific standards for "Knowledge of Language."

CONVENTIONS OF STANDARD ENGLISH

In a study conducted by Partnership for 21st Century Skills (2006) of employers' perspectives of high school graduates' workforce readiness, survey results indicated that 72% of employers thought that high school graduates are deficient in writing (this includes grammar and spelling), while 38.4% thought that graduates are deficient in reading comprehension. Language development provides a strong basis for success with reading and writing. The CCSS for "Conventions of Standard English" establish a foundation for continued language improvement:

1. Demonstrate command of the conventions of standard English grammar and usage when writing or speaking.
2. Demonstrate command of the conventions of standard English capitalization, punctuation, and spelling when writing.

"Grammar glues our language together in a way that makes sense to the speaker and listener when words are placed in the 'right order' of a specific language" (Rothstein & Rothstein, 2009, p. 3). All children learn language from a young age but cannot explain or recite the rules. As Elizabeth Ryan states, "Nobody is born knowing how to speak and write Standard English, just as nobody is born knowing how to talk—by practice and by getting a feel for what sounds right " (2003, "Introduction").

Although "grammar" and "usage" are used interchangeably, they are different. Grammar refers to the formal written rules of language, whereas usage refers to the choice of language one uses, usually when speaking. "The grammar for both speaking and writing that fits this uniform set of rules is known as Standard English" (Ryan, 2003, "Introduction"). However, Allen (2003) believes that learning grammar does not necessarily lead to better writing skills. According to Lindblom and Dunn (2006):

Traditional grammar instruction can encourage distorted views of how language works, ignoring some of the most interesting aspects of language shift and change. Traditional grammar instruction can help to perpetuate cultural prejudices regarding class and race that are mirrored in what is often referred to as the difference between "correct" and "incorrect" or between "proper" and "improper" language use. (p. 71)

Focusing on "correct" grammar and memorizing and reciting grammar rules can turn some students (and teachers) off to grammar learning. It is important to learn about grammar by exploring different ways we use language and by respecting the diversity in languages across cultures and societies. According to Rothstein and Rothstein (2009):

> Using judgmental definitions (rather than descriptive ones) often causes students to feel embarrassed about their own language rather than become inspired to understand language in all its varieties. The focus of language education is to equip the learner with a deep understanding of different forms of language that can be applied to a wide range of circumstances. The tone needs to be additive rather than "corrective." (pp. 11–12)

Dewey would agree that experiential learning—learning the rules of language as they are being used—would contribute to the automatic processing of grammar. Grammar and usage then become second nature, and students apply their knowledge during reading, writing, speaking, and listening without thinking.

Many English teachers and college professors alike have lamented students' lack of command of grammar and usage and even declared the English language dead. Weak grammar skills are seen in college admissions exams and in-class essays across the world. According to Paul Budra, an English professor and associate dean of arts and science at Simon Fraser in Ontario:

> The words "a lot" have become one word, for everyone, as far as I can tell. "Definitely" is always spelled with an "a"—"definately." I don't know why . . . . Punctuation errors are huge, and apostrophe errors. Students seem to have absolutely no idea what an apostrophe is for. (Kelley, 2010, para. 18–19)

Dr. Budra attributes students' poor writing skills to the lack of grammar instruction in schools in the past 30–40 years and the Internet norm of ignoring grammar. Writing "cuz" and "wuz" and inserting smiley faces may be appropriate in e-mail messages to friends but not in formal writing.

According to the Anchor Standards for "Conventions of Standard English," students must "demonstrate command of both the conventions of standard English grammar and usage when writing or speaking and the conventions of standard English capitalization, punctuation, and spelling when writing." However, it seems that common misspellings and incorrect use of the apostrophe can be found everywhere nowadays, including on store signs. For example, the delicatessen near Vicky's house sells "heros." As Donald Graves (1983) stated:

> Spelling is a form of etiquette that shows the writer's concern for the reader. Poor spelling in the midst of a good piece of writing is like attending a lovely banquet but with the leavings of grime and grease

from the previous meal still left on the table. Poor spelling can also show the writer's lack of consideration for the reader. The banquet may be fine but it is tainted by a distracting factor—poor spelling. (p. 183)

Spelling errors and other errors in conventions are becoming more and more commonplace. In fact, it is not surprising anymore to find errors in newspaper articles. According to Weingarten (2010), the English language's demise

had been evident for some time on the pages of America's daily newspapers, the flexible yet linguistically authoritative forums through which the day-to-day state of the language has traditionally been measured. Beset by the need to cut costs, and influenced by decreased public attention to grammar, punctuation and syntax in an era of unedited blogs and abbreviated instant communication, newspaper publishers have been cutting back on the use of copy editing, sometimes eliminating it entirely. (para. 3)

Is today's technology (i.e., blogging, tweeting, texting, instant messaging) contributing to the destruction of language skills among students? Perhaps not. According to Oxford's 2009 Word List, words like "unfriend" (verb: to remove a friend from Facebook) and "Paywall" (noun: a way of blocking access to a part of a website that is only available to paying subscribers) have entered the list. According to Betty Birner of the Linguistic Society of America, "Language is always changing, evolving, and adapting to the needs of its users" (n.d., para. 1). And we in turn need to adapt to it. Some studies have found that students who text message (use abbreviated words and letters to convey words and sentiments) are better spellers and writers; because they are abbreviating and playing with language, they have a better sense of how sounds of the language relate to the letters (Crystal, 2009). Initially, it may seem that technology is wearing away students' grammar and spelling skills, but perhaps, it is changing the way students' skills evolve for the better. This is more likely to be the case if we maintain students' connection to basic rules of grammar and spelling by meeting the CCSS above.

KNOWLEDGE OF LANGUAGE

There is no doubt that technology is rapidly changing the English language. Rather than a threat, perhaps text messaging can be viewed as a dialect or its own separate language, just like any other, that students must understand and use appropriately. Learning new languages does not mean we forget to learn the "old languages." Students must still learn traditional reading, writing, speaking, and listening along with grammar and usage. According to ACT (2010), only 35% of students have sufficient "knowledge of language varieties and ability to use language skillfully" (p. 7). They must understand how to shift their voices to fit various social situations or contexts and how to apply their understanding of context to the interpretation of someone else's language choices. The "Knowledge of Language" Anchor Standard addresses this need:

> 3. Apply knowledge of language to understand how language functions in different contexts, to make effective choices for meaning or style, and to comprehend more fully when reading or listening.

Language is complex and can consist of rules that do not always make sense. Think of the radio commercial for Geico. The actor asks, "How come a 'fat chance' and a 'slim chance' are the same thing, but a 'wise guy' and a 'wise man' are opposites?" Understanding language with its own unique rules, how it functions in different contexts, and how choices affect the meaning of a message are expectations of the CCSS addressed by the Anchor Standards for "Knowledge of Language." In addition to mastering conventions of standard English grammar and usage, students "must come to appreciate that language is as at least as much a matter of craft as of rules and be able to choose words, syntax, and punctuation to express themselves and achieve particular functions and rhetorical effects" (NGA Center/CCSSO, 2010b, p. 51). There is a difference between errors and craft. Writers who choose to use nonstandard English in their writing do so to achieve a particular effect. Knowing when to use what language form is a measure of someone's language and literacy skills.

Dunn and Lindblom (2011) recommend an unconventional way of helping students become aware of grammar issues and learn about language through the use of grammar rants. By analyzing "published complaints of other people's language use" (e.g., run-on sentences, comma splices, misspellings, etc.), students can understand the importance of word choice, question the assumptions and motives of the ranters, examine the validity of the complaints, and become informed about grammar and how it can be used to shape a piece of writing. By examining the rhetorical discourse of rants and discovering the inherent contradictions, the goal is for students to develop skepticism about what they read and, ultimately, confidence in their own writing skills. As a result, their communication skills improve.

The ability to effectively communicate is a prerequisite for college and the workforce. In her book about the skills students will need in higher education and the workplace and the strategies teachers can use to develop their abilities, middle school teacher and author Heather Wolpert-Gawron (2011) lists communication as one of the top five skills. According to a survey by the National Association of Colleges and Employers, the ability to effectively communicate is the most favored skill in the workforce. With companies downsizing and limited jobs available, employers are looking for candidates with strong communication skills who can work well with others (see more about communication in Chapter 6).

VOCABULARY ACQUISITION AND USE

According to ACT (2010), only 35% of students are performing at a college- and career-readiness level regarding vocabulary acquisition (p. 7). The need to improve students' vocabulary is addressed by Standards 4–6, "Vocabulary Acquisition and Use" within the Language strand:

4. Determine or clarify the meaning of unknown and multiple-meaning words and phrases by using context clues, analyzing meaningful word parts, and consulting general and specialized reference materials, as appropriate.

5. Demonstrate understanding of word relationships and nuances in word meanings.

6. Acquire and use accurately a range of general academic and domain specific words and phrases sufficient for reading, writing, speaking, and listening at the college and career readiness level; demonstrate independence in gathering vocabulary knowledge when considering a word or phrase important to comprehension or expression.

Sadly, all too often, if students encounter a word that they do not know, they simply skip it, hoping the rest of what they are reading will make sense. As teachers, we encourage students to use context clues and/or to find a dictionary to help them make sense of meaning; however, that takes a lot of mental effort. Students may ask, "Just skipping the word doesn't really hurt anybody, does it?" The bigger question that teachers need to ask is, "What has happened to make students see vocabulary acquisition as such a chore?" One answer to that question may be the focus on rote memorization. Figgins and Johnson (2007) wrote, "We have found that if students are given permission to play with language, as they once did freely as a child, their relationship with language is likely to change. Teachers, however, must create the context and conditions" (p. 32). How can we step away from oppressive vocabulary routines and into a more light and natural yet meaningful approach to vocabulary?

Isabel Beck and her colleagues (2002) recommend teachers focus mostly on instruction of Tier Two vocabulary words. Tier One words consist of basic words that rarely require addressing; Tier Two words are high-frequency words for sophisticated language users found across knowledge domains; and Tier Three words are of low frequency that are limited to specific knowledge domains. According to Beck and colleagues, "Tier Two words are not only words that are important for students to know, they are also words that can be worked with in a variety of ways so that students have opportunities to build rich representations of them and of their connections to other words and concepts" (p. 20). It is important to build students' vocabulary through instruction of Tier Two words, or academic words, such as *discourse, entrenched, hypothesis,* in order to enable students to access complex text.

If teachers repeatedly use sophisticated language, then when students encounter similar language in their reading, their vocabulary muscles are well-developed. Smith (2008) wrote, "By creating word-rich environments through our vocabulary use . . . , teachers establish their classrooms as word laboratories that encourage students to try out and play with new and unfamiliar words"

(p. 25). "Try out and play"—if the lightheartedness connoted by those words could be applied to vocabulary development, perhaps students would be more invested.

Speaking of connotation, Crovitz and Miller (2008) discussed the need to help students better appreciate the nuances in word meaning as called for in Standard 5. Earlier, Maureen bemoaned the use of words like "nice" and "good" to describe characters. Crovitz and Miller (2008) stated that both students and teachers "[gloss] over important language choices people make regarding *connotative impact.* When this happens, words get reduced to mere placeholders. This means that one synonym is as good as another, the only caveat being that any single word shouldn't be used too often" (p. 49). To help assess the quality of words, Crovitz and Miller designed a matrix on which to plot the positive or negative connotation of words and their formal or informal nature.

Simply considering these factors can have a significant effect on word selection. Crovitz and Miller (2008) argue that "if students can imagine words as not simply occupying slots of permanent meaning but instead evolving over time and governed by context, they are engaging in higher level thinking about what words mean and can do" (p. 53). This kind of consideration would appeal to Bloom. Students travel far beyond basic comprehension to analysis and evaluation. When considering how a word functions in a given format or when used with a specific audience, the concept of application of knowledge becomes highly sophisticated. Dewey would approve of this kind of consideration because the clarity of the word choice allows for better interpersonal relations. The Interpersonal and Verbal-Linguistic aspects of this connect with Gardner as well.

Regarding Standard 6, ACT (2010) stated, "Particularly important is that students gain what the Standards refer to as general academic vocabulary: words and phrases that are often encountered in written texts in a variety of subjects but that are rarely heard in spoken language" (p. 7). Again, teacher modeling plays a strong role in developing meaningful vocabulary knowledge, a good work ethic, and the needed skills for answering vocabulary questions. Content area teachers need to focus on content-specific vocabulary (e.g., metaphor, simile, climax). In addition, teachers and students can take time to consider common academic terms (e.g., *compare, describe, analyze, support*) encountered in school and define/or clarify said terms. Far too often, though, more sophisticated language is found in print than is used by the teacher. Smith (2008) wrote, "While we [teachers] tend to use low-level words almost exclusively, the books we ask students to read do no such thing" (p. 22). As teachers, we must align our vocabulary with one another and with what students are encountering in text. When we raise the vocabulary bar, students will follow.

A CLOSER LOOK

Let's look at the grade-specific standards for "Knowledge of Language." When we examine these standards, we see a clear progression. Grade 6 focuses on varied sentence patterns, while Grade 7 requires students to be selective with the language contained in those varied sentences and Grade 8 focuses on voice and mood. When students reach high school, the standards become more pointed. Students apply the knowledge and skills they have developed to various contexts or purposes. Grade-specific 9–10 standards call for students to conform to style guidelines such as those set by the Modern Language Association. Grade-specific 11–12 standards require even more nuanced skills such as modifying syntax for style and effect.

The scaffolded nature of the grade-specific CCSS would please Bloom. In Grades 6–8, students are developing their *understanding* of specific elements of language (sentence variation, word choice, voice). They *apply* their understanding of language to a given context in Grades 9–10 and they *synthesize* their style with style choices recommended in reference guides in Grades 11–12.

Table 8.2 Language Standards for 6–8 (NGO Center/CCSSO, 2010b, p. 52)

Grade 6 Students	Grade 7 Students	Grade 8 Students
Knowledge of Language	*Knowledge of Language*	*Knowledge of Language*

3. Use knowledge of language and its conventions when writing, speaking, reading, or listening.
  Vary sentence patterns for meaning, reader/listener interest, and style.
  Maintain consistency in style and tone.
	3. Use knowledge of language and its conventions when writing, speaking, reading, or listening.
	  Choose language that expresses ideas precisely and concisely recognizing and eliminating wordiness and redundancy.
		3. Use knowledge of language and its conventions when writing, speaking, reading, or listening.
		  Use verbs in the active and passive voice and in the conditional and subjunctive mood to achieve particular effects (e.g., emphasizing the actor or the action; expressing uncertainty or describing a state contrary to fact).

Table 8.3 Language Standards for 9–12 (NGO Center/CCSSO, 2010b, p. 54)

Grades 9–10 Students	Grades 11–12 Students
Knowledge of Language	*Knowledge of Language*

3. Apply knowledge of language to understand how language functions in different contexts to make effective choices for meaning or style, and to comprehend more fully when reading or listening.
  Write and edit work so that it conforms to the guidelines in a style manual (e.g., *MLA Handbook*, Turabian's *Manual for Writers*) appropriate to the discipline and writing type.
	3. Apply knowledge of language to understand how language functions in different contexts, to make effective choices for meaning or style and to comprehend more fully when reading or listening.
	  Vary syntax for effect, consulting references (e.g., Tufte's *Artful Sentences*) for guidance as needed; apply an understanding of syntax to the study of complex texts when reading.

Obviously, this development of language skills would please Dewey as well. Students who are able to understand the nuances of language and to express themselves well are likely to be productive citizens.

CONCLUSION

The ability to know and apply the conventions of standard English, language, and vocabulary are standards for college and career readiness, according to the CCSS. Some of our students, native speakers, speakers of other varieties of English, and English language learners alike, have difficulty mastering the English language.

Meet Anna, for example. She is an 11th grader. She is articulate and well-spoken and the first to volunteer to present and participate in class activities, especially debates. Anna has dreams of becoming a journalist. Her ability to switch language codes depending on her audience is impressive. She alternates register and vernacular, speaking to some of her classmates and friends in non-standard English ("John backpack is orange"; "cuz I ain't going") and her teachers in formal standard English. As successful as her oral skills are, Anna, nevertheless, does not exhibit the same exemplary communication skills in writing. Her command of written conventions is weak. She exhibits common misspellings and makes errors in capitalization and punctuation. Many of Anna's sentences are run-on, lack subject-verb agreement, and consist of mis-placed modifiers. The message she wants to communicate, usually a good one, is hidden and inhibited by all the errors.

Anna understands that in order to be successful in her career and in life, she needs to improve her written language skills. Anna switches to and from standard and nonstandard English, depending on the situation and listeners she is addressing. Although she speaks without thinking about any rules of grammar, in writing, she needs to be conscious of and follow a set of formal rules. Do you have students like Anna? If so, how do you help them succeed in language? How do you help them learn to express themselves "meaningfully and clearly" (to return to the Cobbett's quote)? How can the CCSS help?

QUESTIONS/CHALLENGES/ PONDERING POINTS

1. How has the 21st century changed your perspective on teaching language?

2. How complex are the language development tasks that you are assigning to your students?

3. In what ways do your students need to improve their language skills?

4. How do you design curriculum that addresses your students' needs for improvement?

5. How do you modify instruction to promote the development of language skills?

9 Language Lessons From the Classroom

INTRODUCTION

In this chapter, we will present three lessons that we believe are particularly effective for addressing the Common Core State Standards (CCSS) for Language. The Grades 6–8 lesson, Literary Devices Booklet, focuses on examining the use of literary devices and how they shape the meaning and style of a literary work. The *Of Mice and Men* Visualization Exercise for Grades 9–10 allows students to explore language and how it functions in Steinbeck's novel. Lastly, in the Grades 11–12 lesson, Speech Analysis, students apply their understanding of rhetorical language and how it functions in a speech by composing their own speeches.

Within the first lesson, Literary Devices Booklet, students analyze how specific word choice in the poem "Stopping by Woods on a Snowy Evening" by Robert Frost shapes the meaning or tone of the poem. Students demonstrate an understanding of literary devices by creating their own literary devices booklet based on a work of literature. In the Visualization Exercise *Of Mice and Men*, students are asked to visualize the setting of Steinbeck's novel and examine how language functions in the story. They write dialogue between the two main characters, George and Lennie, in which they are required to make effective choices for meaning or style. The third lesson, Speech Analysis, is designed to help students identify the rhetorical devices in the speech "I Have a Dream" by Martin Luther King Jr. and Old Major's speech in George Orwell's *Animal Farm*. They examine how speakers use arguments to have a particular impact on their audience. Students demonstrate what they have learned in this lesson by writing and delivering their own argumentative speeches.

In all three lessons, students analyze and use language to understand how it functions in different contexts. They acquire and use vocabulary effectively. As you read through these lessons and as you develop your own lessons, we encourage you to focus on how you can guide your students to meet the CCSS for Language. Two sets of questions for reflection are listed below—specific questions pertaining to Language Anchor Standards and general questions regarding Lesson Design:

LANGUAGE ANCHOR STANDARDS REFLECTIVE QUESTIONS

How does the lesson require students to do one or more of the following?

1. Demonstrate command of the conventions of standard English grammar and usage when writing or speaking?

2. Demonstrate command of the conventions of standard English capitalization, punctuation, and spelling when writing?

3. Apply knowledge of language to understand how language functions in different contexts and how language choice affects meaning?

4. Determine or clarify the meaning of unknown and multiple-meaning words and phrases strategically and independently?

5. Demonstrate understanding of word relationships and nuances in word meanings?

6. Acquire and use accurately a range of general academic and domain-specific words and phrases?

LESSON DESIGN REFLECTIVE QUESTIONS

1. How does the lesson require close and multiple readings of grade-level complex text (classic, contemporary, or informational)?

2. How does my questioning require students to use the text as support for their interpretations/arguments?

3. How does the lesson incorporate varied thinking skills (e.g., read, summarize, analyze, interpret)? (Bloom)

4. How does the lesson include the three components of Backward Design: (a) desired results, (b) acceptable evidence, and (c) learning experiences?

5. How do I differentiate instruction, materials, and expectations for this particular lesson so that struggling students can be successful?

6. How does the lesson provide opportunities for technology/media use?

7. How does the lesson include research-based instructional strategies to promote effective teaching?

8. How can the lesson present opportunities for interdisciplinary connections?

9. How does the lesson provide opportunities for students with varied Multiple Intelligences to be successful? (Gardner)

10. How do I present the lesson in a way that encourages students to see the value of what they are learning (e.g., service learning, college- and career-readiness skills)? (Dewey)

Lesson Plan Template

TOPIC:
Literary Devices Booklet (Grades 6–8)

CCSS STRAND:
Language

TEXTS TYPES AND PURPOSES:
Explain/Inform

TIMING:
4 class periods

BACKWARD DESIGN COMPONENTS:

DESIRED RESULTS/CCSS ADDRESSED:

- Analyze how specific word choices in the poem shape meaning or tone [R.4].
- Strengthen booklets through peer response [W.5].
- Present information contained in booklets appropriately [SL.5].
- Understand how language functions in different contexts and comprehend more fully when reading or listening [L.1].
- Demonstrate understanding of figurative language [L.4] and word choice [L.5].

ACCEPTABLE EVIDENCE:

- Response to Poem
- Literary Devices Booklet
- Presentation of Literary Devices Booklet

LEARNING EXPERIENCES AND INSTRUCTION:

- Day 1—Respond to and analyze poem.
- Day 2—Craft Literary Devices Booklet.
- Day 3—Peer-response to Literary Devices Booklet.
- Day 4—Present Literary Devices Booklet.

STRATEGIES:
- Guidance and Monitoring
- Modeling
- Discussion

- Cooperative Learning
- Writing Process

SUPPLEMENTAL RESOURCES:
- Audio recording of poem

TECHNOLOGY/MEDIA OPPORTUNITIES:

- Listen to several different readings of the poem and discuss how differences in pitch, enunciation, and voice affect the meaning of the poem.
- Present the Literary Devices Booklet using PowerPoint or Prezi.

SERVICE LEARNING LINK:

- Create posters with slogans for sports teams or for school events that include quotes from other poems with appropriate literary devices.
- Write greeting cards with literary devices for distribution at a local hospital or nursing home.

VARIATIONS:

- Use with any other literary text in any genre.
- Complete activity independently using the class text or text of choice.
- As a postproject assignment, students take on the role of poet and apply their understanding of literary devices by writing their own poetry using at least five devices.

LITERARY DEVICES BOOKLET

(Grades 6–8; Explain/Inform)

Vicky Speaks

One semester, I taught a class of students who needed extra support to develop the necessary literacy skills to be successful on the state exam. After weeks of attempting various unsuccessful instructional activities to reach my reluctant learners, I adapted the literary devices booklet project that my colleague, Ms. Maryann Franklin, had successfully used in her classes. The goal of this lesson is twofold: to comprehend and appreciate a literary work; and to examine closely the language of the text (literary devices, e.g., figurative language) [L.1] as well as understand how it functions in different contexts [L.4].

Materials Needed

Coloring pencils/Magazines/Google images

Paper and pens

Handouts

Timing

4 class periods

Day 1—Respond to and analyze poem.

Day 2—Craft Literary Devices Booklet.

Day 3—Peer-response to Literary Devices Booklet.

Day 4—Present Literary Devices Booklet.

Day 1

The lesson is on Robert Frost's (1983) "Stopping by Woods on a Snowy Evening." Students are asked to read (and/or listen to an audio recording of the poem: www.poetryfoundation.org/features/video/18) and respond personally to the poem in writing (**Handout 1**). How does it affect them aesthetically? In other words, how does the poem make them feel? What does it remind them of? What questions does the poem raise for them? What literary devices in the poem (e.g., setting, imagery, rhyme) affect them? What impact does the poet's word choice have on them [L.5]?

 THEORY LINK (Gardner): Appeals to Intrapersonal Intelligence.

For example, they can respond that the image of the solitary traveler and his horse in the woods on a snowy evening creates a sense of peace or serenity. Students share their responses during whole class

THEORY LINK (Bloom): Students *comprehend* and *analyze* the poem.

discussion. We discuss the function of literary devices and why poets decide to use certain literary devices in their poetry. Students make connections between their aesthetic responses and what they think the poem is about. We analyze the poem to understand its meaning and how choices in language affect meaning or style [R.4, L.1].

Day 2

The next assignment requires students to work in groups to create a literary devices booklet that demonstrates understanding of literary devices and how they function in a work of literature (**Handout 2**). They are required to select a minimum of five literary devices in the poem and include several features: (a) a fully developed description of each literary element, (b) a definition, (c) at least one example from the text, (d) the purpose of the use of the element, and (e) a visual aid. They write a conclusion to the booklet explaining which literary devices they selected to write about and why. They also create a title page and an outline that shows what is in the booklet.

As a class, we brainstorm possible literary devices that can be analyzed in the booklets. The brainstorm provides an opportunity to review literary devices

THEORY LINK (Gardner): Appeals to Interpersonal Intelligence.

that have been taught before. Students refer to their literary devices list (**Handout 3**), which they keep in their binders. Students get in their assigned groups and begin listing and deciding which literary devices to focus on for this project. They proceed with the description and analysis of each. I offer my assistance when needed and monitor students' progress.

Day 3

Next, the groups exchange the written texts and engage in peer-response [W.5]. After receiving feedback, they make the necessary revisions on the written texts and submit a final draft.

Day 4

When my students are ready, we spend a class period presenting and discussing the literary devices booklets [SL.5].

TECH CONNECTION: Students could also use PowerPoint, Weebly, or Google Docs for their presentations.

THEORY LINK (Gardner): Appeals to Verbal-Linguistic Intelligence.

The booklets as well as the presentations are evaluated using rubrics (**Handout 4** and **Handout 5**), and I display the booklets to be perused by other group members. All students find this project refreshing and motivating because it appeals to their diverse learning styles and intelligences.

This assignment can be modified in different ways. In groups or individually, students can create booklets based on their own choice of literary works that they have read in class or during independent reading so that a range of texts and genres are represented in our discussion. I have used this assignment successfully with a play that we read as a class as well as different novels that students read during independent practice.

I like the literary devices booklet assignment because it motivates students to become engaged in their reading and deepens their textual comprehension. It allows them to understand the use of literary devices in poetry and thus to examine the poem from the perspective of the poet.

The literary devices booklet assignment helps students become good readers, writers, and thinkers because it focuses on thinking, speaking, listening, analyzing, synthesizing, and creating text.

THEORY LINK (Dewey): Purposeful learning— Students experience what it is like to write like a poet.

HANDOUT 1

RESPONSE TO ROBERT FROST'S "STOPPING BY WOODS ON A SNOWY EVENING"

Directions: Read Robert Frost's "Stopping by Woods on a Snowy Evening." Answer the following questions. (Be prepared to share your responses during the whole class discussion.)

1. What do you think the poem is about? Provide evidence from the poem to support your interpretation.

2. How does the poem make you feel (e.g., apprehensive)? What parts of the poem make you feel the way you do (e.g., My little horse must think it queer/To stop without a farm-house near)?

3. What does the poem make you think about? (What does it remind you of?)

4. Select two literary devices in the poem (e.g., setting, imagery, rhyme). Explain how each contributes to the way you feel about the poem (e.g., the image of the solitary traveler and his horse in the woods on a snowy evening creates a sense of peace or serenity). Consider why the poet may have used it.

   a. Device #1:

      Line from the poem:

      Effect:

   b. Device #2:

      Line from the poem:

      Effect:

5. Circle the three most important words.

   a. Why did the poet use word #1?

   b. Why did the poet use word #2?

   c. Why did the poet use word #3?

6. What questions does the poem raise for you?

HANDOUT 2

LITERARY DEVICES BOOKLET

Directions: You are required to create a booklet of the literary devices we have discussed from "Stopping by Woods on a Snowy Evening" by Robert Frost. You are to select a minimum of 5 literary devices. Follow the guidelines below.

1. **Make a title page** with the following information centered on the page.

   Example: "Stopping by Woods on a Snowy Evening" by Robert Frost

   A Literary Devices Booklet

(In the bottom right corner write: Your first and last name; Class; Date)

2. **Make an outline** that shows what is in the booklet.
   Example:
   - I. Setting
   - II. Characters
   - III. Plot

3. Using one page per literary element, **DESCRIBE FULLY:**
   - The **Definition** of the literary element
   - At least one **Example** from the text and an **Explanation** of the meaning of the example
   - The **Purpose** of the Element (tell how the element affects your understanding or your mood)
   - **A Visual Aid**: A visual aid means anything that shows a visual representation of what you are writing about. Examples might include drawings or pictures from a magazine or Google images, if you are using a computer; use your imagination! (Sample page attached.)

4. Write a conclusion to your booklet. Explain which literary devices you selected to write about and why.

5. In pairs, respond to the booklet. Revise your booklet based on the feedback that you receive during this activity,
   - Be sure your booklet is **neat and legible.** Please type if possible. Your work will be assessed on dimensions that include creativity, color, neatness, and completeness.

6. Present your work to the class.

Good luck!!

SAMPLE LITERARY DEVICES BOOKLET PAGE

IMAGERY

DEFINITION:

A word or phrase that stimulates the senses.

EXAMPLE:

The woods are lovely, dark and deep.

EXPLANATION:

This image describes the setting of the poem depicting quiet and solitude. The peacefulness of the woods is contradicted by the darkness and unknown aspects of the setting.

PURPOSE:

Frost's description of the woods poses a dilemma for the speaker who is enjoying the winter landscape but realizes he needs to move on because he needs to tend to his obligations in life.

HANDOUT 3

LITERARY ELEMENTS/DEVICES

Theme

Definition: Message, repeated lesson

Example:

Character Development

Definition: The way a character changes throughout the work

Example:

Symbolism

Definition: When an object represents a greater meaning

Example:

Mood

Definition: The feelings of the characters—and feelings of the reader

Example:

Tone

Definition: Feelings of the author about the subject matter

Example:

Imagery

Definition: Details create a picture for the reader

Example:

Allusion

Definition: Reference to another work—Bible, history

Example:

Irony

Definition: Strange coincidences (sometimes involving opposites)

Example:

Dramatic Irony

Definition: When readers/viewers know something that a character does not know

Example:

Juxtaposition

Definition: Positioning of ideas for effect

Example:

Diction

Definition: Meaningful word choice

Example:

Simile

Definition: Comparison using "like" or "as"

Example:

Metaphor

Definition: Comparison that does not use "like" or "as"

Example:

Personification

Definition: Giving human attributes to nonhumans

Example:

Conflict

Person vs. Person

Example:

Person vs. Self (inner conflict)

Example:

Person vs. Machine/Object

Example:

Person vs. Nature/Fate

Example:

Person vs. Society

Example:

HANDOUT 4

RUBRIC—LITERARY DEVICES BOOKLET

Dimension	4	3	2	1
Content	Literacy devices are described and fully supported.	Literacy devices are explained and partially supported.	Literary devices are somewhat explained.	Literacy devices are not explained and/or not supported.
Organization	Literary devices booklet is well organized. The booklet is fully complete with all required devices: description, title page, outline, body.	Literary devices booklet is well organized, but one of the parts is weak.	Literary devices booklet is organized, but two of the parts are weak.	Literary devices booklet is not well organized. More than two parts are weak.
Conventions	Demonstrates full control of ELA conventions.	Demonstrates partial control of ELA conventions.	Demonstrates a weak control of ELA conventions.	Demonstrates a lack of control of ELA conventions.
Writing Style	Interesting, engaging, shows evidence of clear and deep thinking and analysis. Varies sentence structure.	Interesting and clearly written.	Clearly written.	Written in a mechanical style, does not engage reader, or is not clearly written.
Visual Appeal	The literary devices booklet has visual appeal and creative and original style.	The literary devices booklet has visual appeal and creative style.	The literary devices booklet includes visuals but does not have appeal.	The literary devices booklet does not include visuals.
Number of Literary Devices Described	At least five literary devices are described.	At least four literary devices are described.	At least three literary devices are described.	At least two literary devices are described.

HANDOUT 5

RUBRIC—ORAL PRESENTATION OF LITERARY DEVICES BOOKLET

Dimension	4	3	2	1
Literary Devices	At least five literary devices are clearly presented.	At least four literary devices are clearly presented.	At least three literary devices are clearly presented.	At least two devices are clearly presented.
Content	Shows a full understanding of literary devices, their use, and purpose.	Shows a good understanding of literary devices, their use, and purpose.	Shows a good understanding of literary devices, their use, and purpose.	Does not seem to understand literary devices, their use, and purpose.
Stays on Topic	Stays on topic all (100%) of the time.	Stays on topic most (90–99%) of the time.	Stays on topic some (75–89%) of the time.	It was hard to tell what the topic was.
Voice	Voice is always clear and audible.	Voice is mostly clear and unhurried.	Voice is sometimes clear and audible.	Voice is rarely clear and audible.
Pace	Pace is unhurried and appropriate.	Pace is mostly unhurried and appropriate.	Pace is sometimes hurried or inappropriate.	Pace is hurried or inappropriate.
Collaboration With Peers	Almost always listens to, shares with, and supports the efforts of others in the group. Tries to keep people working well together.	Usually listens to, shares with, and supports the efforts of others in the group. Does not cause "waves" in the group.	Often listens to, shares with, and supports the efforts of others in the group but sometimes is not a good team member.	Rarely listens to, shares with, and supports the efforts of others in the group. Often is not a good team member.

Lesson Plan Template

TOPIC:

Of Mice and Men Visualization Exercise (Grades 9–10)

CCSS STRAND:

Language

TEXTS TYPES AND PURPOSES:

Convey Experience

TIMING:

2 class periods

BACKWARD DESIGN COMPONENTS:

DESIRED RESULTS/CCSS ADDRESSED:

- Interpret words and phrases as they are used in the novel and analyze how specific word choices shape meaning or tone [R.4].
- Write dialogue about imagined experience [W.3].
- Demonstrate command of the conventions of standard English capitalization, punctuation, and spelling when writing the dialogue between George and Lennie [L.2].
- Apply knowledge of language to understand how Steinbeck's language functions in the novel and to make effective choices for meaning or style when writing the dialogue and completing the Language Matrix [L.3].
- Determine or clarify the meaning of unknown and multiple-meaning words and phrases in the novel by using context clues, analyzing meaningful word parts, and consulting general and specialized reference materials, as appropriate [L.4].

ACCEPTABLE EVIDENCE:

- List-Group-Label activity
- Language Matrix
- Dialogue writing

LEARNING EXPERIENCES AND INSTRUCTION:

- Day 1—Engage in Visualization Exercise.
- Day 2—Write dialogue.
- Day 3—Complete Language Matrix.

STRATEGIES:

- Guidance and Monitoring
- Discussion
- Cooperative Learning

SUPPLEMENTAL RESOURCES:

- Listen to an audio reading of the novel.

TECHNOLOGY/MEDIA OPPORTUNITIES:

- View several versions of the novel in film.
- View adaptations of the story and characters in cinema, theater, and popular culture (music, radio, television, cartoons, and animation).

SERVICE LEARNING LINK:

- Students write their own descriptions of settings that have had an important impact on their lives (e.g., vacation house, recreation center, library) and give these descriptions to the people who go with them to these places or to the people who run these places.
- Students interview local senior citizens about settings that have been important to them. They publish brief narrative descriptions or poems based on their findings and share at a luncheon or display in a public area (library, bank, town hall).

VARIATIONS:

- Each group of students can be assigned a different sense that they focus on during the visualization exercise. All five groups share their responses.
- Students can act out their dialogue or record it and play it back to the class.
- One pair can act out its own dialogue and another pair can act out the dialogue in the novel for comparison.
- Groups can rotate dialogues and comment on them in writing.

LANGUAGE LESSON FROM THE CLASSROOM: *OF MICE AND MEN* VISUALIZATION EXERCISE

(Grades 9–10; Convey Experience)

Vicky Speaks

When I first began teaching *Of Mice and Men* (1937) by John Steinbeck, I found that students were reluctant to read what they considered to be the long, descriptive opening of the story that creates an image of the natural setting. I knew I needed to help them appreciate this beginning passage for the language but also its importance to the plot of the story. The setting of the river is important because it sets the stage for the story and ends it as well. This is where we find George and Lennie talking about the past and making plans for the future when the story opens; it is also the spot where Lennie's life tragically ends by the hand of his friend, George. I decided to use a visualization exercise to hook students into the story and provide them with a rich linguistic experience. I found the alternate version of the setting used for the visualization exercise in a curriculum guide at my high school and have used it over the years in different ways.

Materials Needed

Copy of *Of Mice and Men* by John Steinbeck

Interactive whiteboard

Paper and pens

Handouts

Timing

2 class periods

Day 1—Engage in Visualization Exercise.

Day 2—Write dialogue.

Day 3—Complete Language Matrix.

Day 1

On the first day of this lesson, I ask students to close their eyes and listen to a passage that I will read to them (**Handout 1**), have a sensory experience, and try to recall as much as they can at the end of the reading. I do not tell students on which story the setting is based because I want students to focus on the language, experience the setting for themselves, and reconstruct what they think the setting is like and how it might relate to a story that they will be reading. At the end of the reading, I ask students to take a couple of minutes and jot down

DIFFERENTIATION TIP: Students can have the option of completing this activity in groups.

words, phrases, and images that they remember from the reading.

I then elicit their responses and display them on the interactive whiteboard. We engage in an adapted List-Group-Label activity. This is a three-step labeling and grouping process that helps students improve their vocabulary and organizational skills:

1. List key words from a selection

2. Categorize the key words based on shared characteristics in groups

3. Label the groups

TECH CONNECTION: Students can post their responses on the interactive whiteboard.

After I have elicited most or all responses, I ask students to categorize the responses according to the five senses: Sight, Hearing, Smell, Taste, and Feeling.

In this lesson, I provide the labels instead of having students come up with their own because I want the focus to be on the sensory experience. They come up with responses such as the following:

Sight: deep and green river; golden foothill slopes; yellow sand; leaves under the trees; beaten path; sycamore trees; willow trees; smooth, horizontal limb; ash pile

Hearing: the water running by; lizard skittering; distant voices

Smell: ash; crisp air

Feeling: warm water; hot sand beneath feet

Taste: salty water; gritty, crunchy sand

Often, it is easier for students to describe what they see and hear than what they smell, feel, and taste. They will say something like, "But I don't smell anything." With a few guiding questions, they try to imagine what some of these elements in the setting smell, feel, and taste like and connect them to their prior knowledge. Most, if not all students, have been to a beach before, so what does sand taste like? Or what does hot sand feel like?

THEORY LINK (Gardner): Appeals to Multiple Intelligences.

After students review the groups, they are then asked to predict the location and time of the story and also think about what mood the sensory details evoke. We enter a discussion about mood, what it is and does, and students usually state that the mood in the opening of the story seems peaceful and serene, yet eerie because of unanswered questions: Why is the river water green? Does that signify contamination? Who comes to this location and makes fires and why? Discussing the mood allows me to ask students to predict what they think this story is about based on the visualization exercise and our discussion. They recall from the visualization exercise that the location is in the Salinas River, Soleded. I point out the word in the passage, *Soledad,* and ask students to think about what it means and how it might relate to the theme of the story. This is a great opportunity for me to get my Spanish speakers to offer their knowledge of the Spanish language and define the word (definition: loneliness or solitude). My non-Spanish speakers are encouraged to identify a known word in *Soledad* (sole: solitary; only one). Students come to the conclusion through this lesson that the story that they will be reading is about the theme of loneliness.

The time is probably the past because of the frequent building of fires near the river, something not commonly practiced today. Is this a stopping ground for passersby? For whom exactly? (Eventually, after reading a few pages into the novel, I ask students to infer when the story takes place. The knowledge that the time is during the Great Depression clarifies why characters and events are portrayed the way they are: poor, disadvantaged ranch men struggling to make a living while holding on to the unrealistic dream of one day owning their own land.) It is important to note that all of these interpretations are based on Steinbeck's description of setting. We have not yet heard a description of the approaching men or a line of dialogue.

 DIFFERENTIATION TIP: Students may opt to draw the setting and provide a visual interpretation of it.

Day 2

The next assignment involves a creative activity that will deepen students' understanding of the setting and how it relates to the plot and theme of the story by having them write their own dialogue. We read a brief description of the two main characters, George and Lennie, in Chapter 1 and pay close attention to the choice of words Steinbeck uses to describe the characters [R.4]: "Both men were dressed in denim clothes," "wore black, shapeless hats." George "was small and quick, dark of face, with restless eyes and sharp, strong features" ("small, strong hands, slender arms, a thin and bony nose"). Lennie was a "huge man, shapeless of face, with large, pale eyes, with wide, sloping shoulders" who "walked heavily, dragging his feet a little, the way a bear drags his paws" (Steinbeck, 1937, p. 2). He "flung himself down and drank from the surface of the green pool," "snorting into the water like a horse" (Steinbeck, 1937, p. 3). Steinbeck compares Lennie to an animal: a bear, a horse. George is uneasy about his friend's drinking from the river water, as he "stepped nervously behind him" (Steinbeck, 1937, p. 3). Students get into groups and write a brief dialogue between the two men that enter the scene [W.3]. They are required to use correct conventions in standard English [L.2]. Grading guidelines are used to evaluate the written dialogue (**Handout 2**).

After students are done, they present their dialogues to the rest of the class. Students present the

 DIFFERENTIATION TIP: Students may work on the dialogue in pairs or groups.

THEORY LINK (Dewey):
Purposeful learning—
Students experience for
themselves what it is like to
write like an author.

men as opposite characters: George is small, quick, and smart and Lennie is large, slow, and awkward. Students may note that they are like Timon and Pumbaa from *The Lion King*. We get into a discussion about tone, and students observe that Steinbeck describes the setting and characters in an authentic, realistic way.

After this sharing, we are ready to begin reading the novel and compare the setting description with the modified version that the students have already heard [L.3]. Were key ideas conveyed? Were important terms repeated? How does reading the passage compare with listening to it? We discuss unknown words, use context clues, and refer to dictionaries to figure out word meanings [L.4]. As we continue reading the novel, we also compare the dialogue in Chapter 1 and the dialogue that students constructed. It is interesting to note though that some students create dialogue that is somewhat similar to that of George and Lennie.

THEORY LINK (Bloom):
Students *comprehend* and
analyze the two dialogues.

Day 3

One common difference among the students' writing and Steinbeck's is diction. Both George and Lennie use words or phrases that show they are unrefined ranchers such as "ain't," "kinda," "You'd drink out of a gutter if you was thirsty" (Steinbeck, 1937, p. 3). At this point, students focus on the opening passage and use the Language Matrix (Crovitz & Miller, 2008) (**Handout 3**) to plot the positive or negative connotations of the words in the text and their formal or informal nature. For example, George's character uses words and phrases with negative and informal connotations that reveal the gruff harshness of his character—"You're a crazy bastard" (p. 4) along with his reluctant (at times), but genuine concern for Lennie—"I ain't taking it away jus' for meanness. That mouse ain't fresh Lennie. . . . You get another mouse that's fresh and I'll let you keep it a little while" (p. 9). Lennie's character's voice is still informal and clearly more childlike—"I was only foolin', George. I don't want no ketchup. I wouldn't eat no ketchup if it was right here beside me" (p. 12). By analyzing Steinbeck's diction, students understand how word choice and phrasing can affect character development [R.4].

The passage in which George tells the story of the ranch that he and Lennie will share strongly highlights Steinbeck's skill with both descriptive language and diction [L.3]. The description of the ranch has a dreamlike quality and the fluent rhythm of the language reflects George's telling of the story many times. Lennie's interruptions second this notion of repetition and again, highlight the nature of his character. After reading through the end of the chapter, students can compare how they envisioned the start of the story based on the setting, mood, and tone with how Steinbeck used said components to start his own story. They can also compare their characters' use of language in their dialogue with Steinbeck's writing.

This lesson encourages students to mentally visualize the setting of a story before even reading it. This serves not only as a motivation but also as a way to advance their reading comprehension and their understanding of how language affects meaning. Students must pay close attention to the sensory details of the opening passages in each chapter and how they are significant to the rest of the story. They are encouraged to consider the use of descriptive language and how it affects their ability to identify the setting and mood of the story and predict what the story is about. By anticipating dialogue and plot, students' motivation and comprehension both increase. They are able to consider how language choices create formal versus informal voice or tone. More importantly, students have a multisensory experience of the story, which is always much richer than just reading the words on a page.

TECH CONNECTION: The two dialogues can be presented side-by-side for comparison (on an overhead projector or PowerPoint or interactive whiteboard).

HANDOUT 1

VISUALIZATION EXERCISE

(Based on opening of the novel Of Mice and Men)

Close your eyes. **(Pause)**

Sit back, relax in your chair. **(Pause)** Take a couple of deep breaths. **(Pause)** Let all of the tension out of your body. **(Pause)** You are a few miles south of Soledad in California. The Salinas River runs close by. **(Pause)** It is deep and green. **(Pause)** See the river. Hear the water running by. **(Pause)** On one side of the river see the golden foothill slopes curving up to the strong and rocky mountains. **(Pause)** On the other side see a valley with willow trees and sycamore trees lining the river. **(Pause)**

Move close to the river. **(Pause)** Reach down and feel the warm water running past. **(Pause)** If you are wearing them, take your shoes and socks off. **(Pause)** Feel the hot sand beneath your feet. **(Pause)** Look down and see the yellow sand. **(Pause)** See leaves lying deep under the trees covering the sandy bank. **(Pause)** Hear a lizard skittering across the crisp leaves. Try to see it before it hides under a rock or the leaves. **(Pause)**

Now you notice a path through the willows and among the sycamores. **(Pause)** The path is beaten hard by people and animals who were there before you. **(Pause)** Near the path by the river is a giant sycamore. From it hangs a low horizontal limb. **(Pause)** Look at the ash pile in front of the low horizontal limbs. **(Pause)** It is made by many fires. **(Pause)** The limb is worn smooth by men who have sat on it. Feel the smoothness of the limb. **(Pause)** Now hear the distant voices of two men approaching. **(Pause)**

Now, in a moment, I want you to open your eyes. **(Pause)** Begin to open your eyes now.

HANDOUT 2

OF MICE AND MEN: OPENING DIALOGUE

Grading Guidelines

Sensory Details (30 points) _____

The dialogue incorporates a discussion of at least three sensory details discussed yesterday.

- **Sight:** deep and green river; golden foothill slopes; yellow sand; leaves under the trees; beaten path; sycamore trees; willow trees; smooth, horizontal limb; ash pile
- **Hearing:** the water running by; lizard skittering; distant voices
- **Smell:** ash; crisp air
- **Feeling:** warm water; hot sand beneath feet
- **Taste:** salty water; gritty, crunchy sand

   27–30=excellent, 24–26=good, 21–23=fair, 18–20=poor, <18=failing

Mood (30 points) _____

The dialogue aligns with the mood established by the setting.

- Consider sensory details again
- Consider the time period (The Great Depression)
- Remember that *Soledad* means loneliness

   27–30=excellent, 24–26=good, 21–23=fair, 18–20=poor, <18=failing

Character Description (20 points) _____

The dialogue is believable coming from the men as described by Steinbeck.

- **"Both men** were dressed in denim clothes," "wore black, shapeless hats."
- **George** "was small and quick, dark of face, with restless eyes and sharp, strong features" ("small, strong hands, slender arms, a thin and bony nose").
- **Lennie** was a "huge man, shapeless of face, with large, pale eyes, with wide, sloping shoulders" who "walked heavily, dragging his feet a little, the way a bear drags his paws" (Steinbeck, 1937, p. 2).

   18–20=excellent, 16–19=good, 14–15=fair, 12–13=poor, <12=failing

Conventions (20 points) _____

The dialogue demonstrates command of the conventions of standard English.

–capitalization
–punctuation
–spelling

18–20=excellent, 16–19=good, 14–15=fair, 12–13=poor, <12=failing

TOTAL _____

HANDOUT 3

VOCABULARY MATRIX

Plot the language in Chapter 1 of the novel *Of Mice and Men* on the following matrix. Some examples are given to help you.

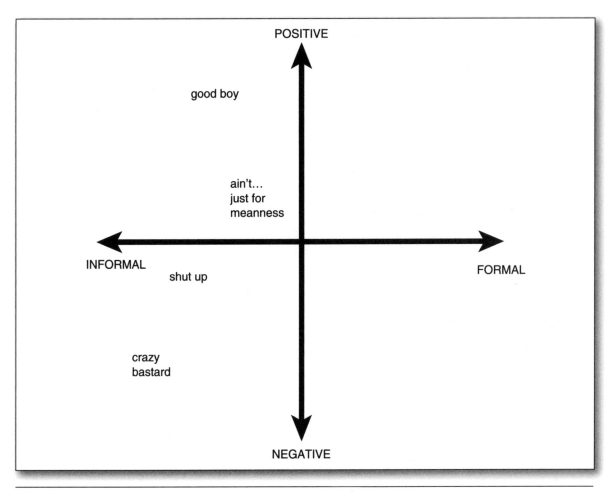

Source: Crovitz, D., & Miller, J. A. (2008, March). Register and charge: Using synonym maps to explore connotation. *English Journal*, 97(4), 49–55.

Lesson Plan Template

TOPIC:
Speech Analysis (Grades 11–12)

PURPOSE/TYPE OF WRITING:
Argue/Persuade

CCSS STRAND:
Reading

TIMING:
3 class periods

BACKWARD DESIGN COMPONENTS:

DESIRED RESULTS/CCSS ADDRESSED:

- Identify and evaluate the arguments as well as the reasoning and evidence in each speech (Dr. King's and Old Major's in *Animal Farm*) [R.8].

- Compare the two speeches [R.9].

- Write coherent argumentative speech using valid reasoning and sufficient evidence and appropriate to task, purpose, and audience [W.1, W.4].

- Strengthen speech through peer-response [W.5].

- Present speech with sound reasoning, organization, and development [SL.4].

- In presentation of speech, demonstrate command of the conventions of standard English, grammar, and usage [L.1].

- Apply knowledge of rhetorical devices to understand how they function in a speech; to make effective choices of rhetorical language in student-created speech; to comprehend assigned speeches when reading and listening [L.3].

ACCEPTABLE EVIDENCE:

- Political Speech Analysis Chart

- Student speeches using rhetorical devices

LEARNING EXPERIENCES AND INSTRUCTION:

- Day 1—Discuss rhetorical devices and analyze Old Major's speech using chart.

- Day 2—Analyze Dr. King's speech and compare with Old Major's speech using chart.

- Day 3—Draft student-created speeches.

- Day 4—Peer-response and revise.

- Days 5–6—Present speeches.

STRATEGIES:
- Guidance and Monitoring
- Modeling
- Discussion
- Writing Process

SUPPLEMENTAL RESOURCES:

- Other historical and presidential speeches (www.americanrhetoric .com/top100speechesall.html; www .history.com/sports-speeches)

TECHNOLOGY/MEDIA OPPORTUNITIES:

- View or listen to speeches by important historical and political figures (consider arguments, line of reasoning, tone of voice, gestures, pace of speaking, etc.).

- Students record their own speeches and replay them in class.

SERVICE LEARNING LINK:

- Students become speech writing consultants for younger students who are developing their campaign speeches for Student Council.

VARIATIONS:

- Use with various genres of speeches (presidential; war; sports) by other authors (e.g., Gettysburg Address; President Obama's Inaugural Address; Dying Babe Ruth's Address to Fans) (www.history.com/sports-speeches).

SPEECH ANALYSIS

(Grades 11–12; Argue/Persuade)

Vicky Speaks

This lesson is designed to help students identify and use rhetorical devices in speeches by examining how speakers use arguments to convince their audiences to act, change their points of view, or accept the reasonableness of their arguments. An argument is a sound, logical way of making a point. The lesson requires that students think deeply about and understand the way that rhetoric works and the powerful role it can play in our lives. In the end, I want students to demonstrate what they have learned in this lesson by writing and delivering their own argumentative speeches.

Materials Needed

Audiorecording, videorecording, and transcript of Martin Luther King Jr.'s speech

Audiorecording and videorecording of Old Major's speech

Animal Farm

Paper and pens

Handouts

Timing

6 class periods

Day 1—Discuss rhetorical devices and analyze Old Major's speech using chart.

Day 2—Analyze Dr. King's speech and compare with Old Major's speech using chart.

Day 3—Draft student-created speeches.

Day 4—Peer-response and revise student-created speeches.

Days 5–6—Present speeches.

Day 1

We have finished reading Chapter 1 of *Animal Farm* (1951) by George Orwell and we are ready to delve deep into the meaning of Old Major's speech. I want students to understand how a speaker uses rhetorical devices to convince others of his or her particular point of view [L.3]. As a motivation, I have students do an improvisation in which they try to persuade someone to do something. I use improvisations a lot in my lessons before, during, or after reading a text because it forces students to think on the spot more deeply and extensively about the reading. It gets all students involved in the learning process by giving them opportunities to create script as they go along in a fun and risk-free way. There are no lines to rehearse, so students feel safe to participate. I ask for volunteers to serve as either a speaker or a listener.

The speaker is given a card that describes the task. For example, the card might state, "You do not agree with the school rule that prohibits the use of cell phones. Come up with at least three arguments or grounds and use them to convince your principal to change this rule." The listener decides whether or not to do what he or she wants as well as to justify the decision. I model the activity first for students and then have two or more pairs improvise. Students enjoy improvising and at the same time learn to identify rhetorical devices and their impact on an audience. For example, the simile, "using cell phones in school is like having hand tools at your disposal and not being able to use them," helps the listener visualize and in turn understand more clearly the value of using cell phones in school; the alliteration "cell phone use in the classroom can enhance education in this era of accountability" creates fluency in the voice of the speaker; and in this case the word choice allows for more formal tone. I distribute a list of rhetorical devices with definitions on a handout. A comprehensive list of rhetorical devices with definitions as well as audio and video recordings is available at www.americanrhetoric.com/figures/anaphora.htm.

After this motivation, students listen to Old Major's speech on audio two or three times and get into groups to identify the rhetorical devices on a graphic organizer (**Handout 1**). After students are done, we review and discuss how Old Major's speech appeals to history and tradition and leads the animals to rebel. Students have an opportunity to make changes to their responses and complete the boxes that they left blank.

Day 2

On the second day, students listen to Martin Luther King Jr.'s "I Have a Dream" speech (delivered on August 28, 1963). They should have read this speech in 10th grade, but for those who did not, we reread and re-listen to it on audio and discuss the context of the speech. Students get into groups again to complete the part of the chart that pertains to Dr. King's speech. After students complete this part, I show a few minutes of a video recording of King's speech and Old Major's speech and ask students to record their thoughts on the delivery of each speech.

THEORY LINK (Gardner): Appeals to Visual-Spatial Intelligence.

THEORY LINK (Bloom): Students exhibit *comprehension* of rhetorical devices and engage in *analysis* and *comparison* of speeches.

Students are quick to note that King's shaking of his head as if in disbelief gives more credibility to his arguments. After analyzing each speech, students are ready to compare the speeches by King and Old Major [R.8, R. 9] on the assigned chart.

One of the comparisons includes both speakers' call for action: King incites people to use "soul force" and resist prejudicial injustice and Old Major calls for an actual, physical rebellion. They each write a comparison paragraph at the bottom of the chart.

I monitor and guide students in the completion of the chart as well as the activities that follow that involve speech writing and presenting.

Day 3

After analyzing the rhetorical devices in two speeches, students are now ready to write their own speech following the appropriate structure and using rhetorical devices [W.1, W.4] (**Handout 2**). They can select any topic as long as it is approved by the teacher.

Day 4

Students are placed in pairs to respond to each other's speeches (**Handout 3**) [W.5]. I sit with each pair and provide my feedback. Students practice delivering their speeches with their partners. They must demonstrate elements of effective speaking (e.g., sound reasoning, coherence), which include conventions of standard English [L.1].

Days 5–6

Students deliver their speeches to the entire class and the audience provides feedback [SL.4]. Discussion ensues regarding the effectiveness of the speeches.

DIFFERENTIATION TIP: Struggling learners can be provided with a partially completed chart and/or be assigned fewer boxes in the chart to complete.

DIFFERENTIATION TIP: Advanced students are given the option of writing an essay or analyzing a more contemporary speech; for instance, Lady Gaga's speech on gays serving in the military.

THEORY LINK (Dewey): Purposeful learning— Students connect lesson to life experience by writing their own speeches.

DIFFERENTIATION TIP: Struggling learners can be heterogeneously grouped.

THEORY LINK (Gardner): Appeals to Interpersonal Intelligence.

THEORY LINK (Bloom): Students *evaluate* each other's speeches.

TECH CONNECTION: Students have the option of presenting their speeches on a podcast.

HANDOUT 1

RHETORICAL DEVICES

Alliteration: repetition of the same sound beginning several words in sequence.

> Veni, vidi, vici.
>
> —Julius Caesar

Anaphora: the repetition of a word or phrase at the beginning of successive phrases, clauses or lines.

> We shall not flag or fail. We shall go on to the end. We shall fight in France, we shall fight on the seas and oceans, we shall fight with growing confidence and growing strength in the air . . .
>
> —Winston Churchill

Antithesis: opposition, or contrast of ideas or words in a balanced or parallel construction.

> Extremism in defense of liberty is no vice, moderation in the pursuit of justice is no virtue.
>
> —Barry Goldwater

Archaism: use of an older or obsolete form.

> Pipit *sate* upright in her chair.
>
> —T. S. Eliot

Assonance: repetition of the same sound in words close to each other.

> Thy kingdom come, thy will be done.
>
> —Matthew 6

Climax: arrangement of words, phrases, or clauses in an order of ascending power. Often the last emphatic word in one phrase or clause is repeated as the first emphatic word of the next.

> One equal temper of heroic hearts,
> Made weak by time and fate, but strong in will
> To strive, to seek, to find, and not to yield.
>
> —Lord Alfred Tennyson

Euphemism: substitution of an agreeable or at least nonoffensive expression for one whose plainer meaning might be harsh or unpleasant.

" . . . burned beyond recognition," which anyone who had been around an air base very long (fortunately Jane had not) realized was quite an artful euphemism to describe a human body that now looked like an enormous fowl that has burned up in a stove.

—Tom Wolfe

Hyperbole: exaggeration for emphasis or for rhetorical effect.

My vegetable love should grow Vaster than empires, and more slow.

—Andrew Marvell

Irony: expression of something that is contrary to the intended meaning; the words say one thing but mean another.

Yet Brutus says he was ambitious;
And Brutus is an honourable man.

—William Shakespeare

Metaphor: implied comparison achieved through a figurative use of words; the word is used not in its literal sense, but in one analogous to it.

Life's but a walking shadow; a poor player,
That struts and frets his hour upon the stage.

—William Shakespeare

Metonymy: substitution of one word for another that it suggests.

The pen is mightier than the sword.

—Edward Bulwer-Lytton

Onomatopoeia: use of words to imitate natural sounds; accommodation of sound to sense.

At tuba terribili sonitu taratantara dixit.

—Ennius

Oxymoron: apparent paradox achieved by the juxtaposition of words that seem to contradict one another.

I must be cruel only to be kind.

—William Shakespeare

Paradox: an assertion seemingly opposed to common sense, but that may yet have some truth in it.

What a pity that youth must be wasted on the young.

—George Bernard Shaw

Personification: attribution of personality to an impersonal thing.

England expects every man to do his duty.

—Lord Nelson

Simile: an explicit comparison between two things using "like" or "as."

Reason is to faith as the eye to the telescope.

—D. Hume

Synecdoche: the use of a part for the whole, or the whole for the part (a form of metonymy).

Give us this day our daily bread.

—Matthew 6

Source: www.uky.edu/AS/Classics/rhetoric.html.

HANDOUT 2

POLITICAL SPEECH ANALYSIS CHART

Directions. In the chart below, compare Martin Luther King Jr.'s speech and Old Major's speech in terms of structure, rhetorical devices, and delivery. Find examples from each speech and include the line numbers and the page numbers where the sources are located.

Structure	"I Have a Dream" (line # and pg. #)	Old Major's Speech (line # and pg. #)
Introduction How does the speaker introduce his speech?		
Narration What are some facts of the current situation? Who is benefiting? Who is suffering?		
Proposition What would life be like if the conditions were different?		
Proof What arguments does the speaker list to make his points?		
Refutation How does the speaker refute the arguments presented against him?		
Conclusion How does the speaker end his speech?		
Rhetorical Devices	"I Have a Dream" (line # and pg. #)	Old Major's Speech (line # and pg. #)
Imagery What are some vivid words or phrases that convey mental imagery? (e.g., "valley of despair")		
Repetition What are some words or phrases that are repeated for emphasis?		
Alliteration What are some sounds that are repeated? (e.g., dignity and discipline)		

(Continued)

(Continued)

Structure	"I Have a Dream" (line # and pg. #)	Old Major's Speech (line # and pg. #)

Metaphor
  What are some comparisons that are used to convey meaning visually?
  (e.g., "great beacon light of hope")		

Rhetorical Questions
  What are some questions that are asked for effect and for which there are no answers?
  (e.g., "What is the nature of this life of ours")		

Allusion
  What are some historical or literary references?
  (e.g., Emancipation Proclamation)		

Delivery	**"I Have a Dream"** (line # and pg. #)	**Old Major's Speech** (line # and pg. #)
What are some gestures and facial expressions? What is the tone of the speech? (e.g., conversational, energetic)		

Conclusion: What can we conclude about the two speeches? How do they compare and contrast? What effect does each one have on the audience? What makes an effective speech?

HANDOUT 2

WRITE YOUR OWN SPEECH

Write your own speech with the purpose of motivating your audience to act. For example, you are writing a speech to convince the principal to let students go out of the building for lunch. In your speech, make sure you include the following:

I. Structure

Introduction: Introduce your speech

Narration: Present some facts of the current situation. Who is benefitting? Who is suffering?

Proposition: Propose a solution to make conditions better.

Proof: Provide arguments to make your points.

Refutation: Refute the arguments presented (that may be presented) against you.

Conclusion: Conclude your speech by (a) summing up, (b) amplifying your position to move the audience to indignation or enthusiasm, or (c) appealing to the audience's emotions.

II. Rhetorical Devices

In addition, use at least four examples of rhetorical devices from the following list:

imagery, repetition, alliteration, metaphor, rhetorical questions, allusion

Select examples that will provide the desired effect.

III. Delivery

In terms of your delivery, think about your gestures and facial expressions as well as the tone of your speech.

HANDOUT 3

PEER-RESPONSE WORKSHEET

I. Structure

1. Does the speech have an introduction?   Yes   No
   If yes, what is it?

2. Does the speech have a narration?   Yes   No
   If yes, what facts are presented?

3. Does the speech have a proposition?   Yes   No
   If yes, what is it?

4. Does the speech have a refutation?   Yes   No
   If yes, what is it?

5. Does the speech have proof?   Yes   No
   If yes, what are the arguments?

6. Does the speech have a conclusion?   Yes   No
   If yes, what is it?

II. Rhetorical Devices

Are at least four examples of rhetorical devices included?   Yes   No
      If yes, which ones?

HANDOUT 4

PRESENTATION RUBRIC

CATEGORY	4	3	2	1
Structure of Speech— Major Components	Speech includes all six major components: introduction, narration, proposition, refutation, proof, conclusion	Speech includes five major components	Speech includes four major components	Speech includes three or fewer components
Structure of Speech— Development and Organization	Speech is fully developed and organized	Speech is satisfactorily developed and organized	Speech is partially developed and organized	Speech is minimally developed and organized
Structure of Speech— Supporting Evidence	Provides supporting evidence clearly and fully	Satisfactorily provides supporting evidence	Partially provides supporting evidence	Minimally provides supporting evidence
Structure of Speech— Coherence	Exhibits an exemplary logical and coherent structure	Exhibits satisfactorily a logical and coherent structure	Exhibits partial coherence and cohesiveness	Exhibits minimal coherence and cohesiveness
Rhetorical Devices	Uses four or more rhetorical devices effectively	Uses three rhetorical devices effectively	Uses two rhetorical devices effectively	Uses one rhetorical device effectively or none at all
Style and Tone of Speech	Style and tone are extremely fitting to task, purpose, and audience	Style and tone are satisfactorily appropriate to task, purpose, and audience	Style and tone are partially appropriate to task, purpose, and audience	Style and tone are minimally appropriate to task, purpose, and audience
Stays on Topic	Stays on topic all (100%) of the time	Stays on topic most (90–99%) of the time	Stays on topic some (80–89%) of the time	It was hard to tell what the topic was

(Continued)

(Continued)

CATEGORY	4	3	2	1
Uses Complete Sentences	Always (99–100% of time) speaks in complete sentences	Mostly (80–98%) speaks in complete sentences	Sometimes (70–79%) speaks in complete sentences	Rarely speaks in complete sentences
ELA Conventions	Demonstrates full control of ELA conventions when speaking	Demonstrates satisfactory control of ELA conventions when speaking	Demonstrates partial control of ELA conventions when speaking	Demonstrates minimal control of ELA conventions when speaking
Posture and Eye Contact	Stands up straight, looks relaxed and confident; establishes eye contact with everyone in the room during the presentation	Stands up straight and establishes eye contact with everyone in the room during the presentation	Sometimes stands up straight and establishes eye contact	Slouches and/or does not look at people during the presentation
Speaks Clearly	Speaks clearly and distinctly all (100%) the time	Speaks clearly and distinctly all (95–99%) the time	Speaks clearly and distinctly most (85–94%) of the time	Often mumbles or cannot be understood
Preparedness	Student is completely prepared and has obviously rehearsed	Student seems pretty prepared but might have needed a couple more rehearsals	The student is somewhat prepared, but it is clear that rehearsal was lacking	Student does not seem at all prepared to present
Listens to Other Presentations	Listens intently; does not make distracting noises or movements	Listens intently but has one distracting noise or movement	Sometimes does not appear to be listening but is not distracting	Sometimes does not appear to be listening and has distracting noises or movements
Evaluates Peers	Answers all three evaluation questions when evaluating each peer (structure, rhetorical devices, delivery)	Answers two evaluation questions when evaluating each peer (structure, rhetorical devices, delivery)	Answers one evaluation question when evaluating each peer (structure, rhetorical devices, delivery)	Answers no evaluation question when evaluating each peer (structure, rhetorical devices, delivery)

Raising the Roof 10

Collaboration Beyond the School Building

COLLABORATION ON CCSA-BASED ELA CURRICULUM DESIGN

In this chapter, we will discuss how we benefited from collaborating on this book, the value of collaboration within our own schools and communities, and the evolution of partnerships prompted by technology. In the past, collaboration was limited; teachers primarily worked with others in their buildings. Now technology has raised the roof, broadening our potential partners for collaboration to far beyond the school building. The Internet allows teachers to connect with fellow educators and content experts (journalists, scientists, historians, etc.) regardless of location. The Common Core State Standards (CCSS) for English Language Arts (ELA) provide a common set of expectations for students across the country, and technology provides a means by which teachers throughout the country can work together to design lessons that incorporate these expectations.

COLLABORATION ON LESSON DESIGN AND WRITING—OUR REFLECTION

We admit it. Collaboration means more work. The adage that two heads are better than one is true; however, in our experience writing and collaborating on designing lessons for this book, we found that two heads thinking about the same topic did not mean that we got to divide the work and walk away with half the pressure or apply half the time to our process. Quite the opposite: We established common goals, were involved in shared decision making, assumed equal responsibility for the work, and maintained communication throughout the entire process. In fact, we were constantly contacting each other, promising to only take a minute to discuss an issue or concern. As New Yorkers, we are acutely aware of the speed of a New York minute—never did we have one of those! Rather, our conversations ran long as we invariably began to think more deeply about the issue at hand. We had meaningful discussions about the efficacy of our standards-based lessons in which we questioned ourselves and constantly considered the students these lessons would affect. We did this in ways that we likely would not have without the additional person questioning, challenging, and praising our choices, our thoughts, and our clarity in conveying our ideas. Like any good partnership in life, we worked hard to establish and maintain a successful collegial relationship based on a good work ethic, shared commitment, and communication. In the end, we feel that we have both become better teachers and better writers because of our collaboration.

Collaboration has been called the number one most important factor in sustaining a professional learning community (DuFour & Eaker, 1998) in which the entire school works together to ensure student success. Discussing issues that focus on teaching and learning leads to the professional growth of the teachers and the academic achievement of the students. In fact, evidence indicates that teacher collaboration contributes to student success (Goddard, Goddard, & Taschannen-Moran, 2007; Schmoker, 1999). According to the guide *Turning Around Chronically Low-Performing Schools* published by the U.S. Department of Education, teacher collaboration was a common approach to improving instruction in the case studies of 35 chronically low-performing schools: In some case studies, teachers shared common planning time, participated in workshops on using data to inform practice, and received regular support from another staff member (e.g., reading teacher, literacy coach, etc.); in another study, teachers reported that the experience of collaboration was personally rewarding as they worked together on planning lessons and aligning them with standards across grade levels (National Center for Education Evaluation and Regional Assistance [NCERA]/Institute of Education Sciences [IES], 2008). In fact, teachers working together in a professional capacity who are involved in decision making and establish solid collegial relationships report greater job satisfaction (Futernick, 2007).

Our experiences of collaborating on this book provide additional support to the research cited above. Working through this writing process provided not only job satisfaction but proved to be what Bloom would call "a difficult pleasure." We enjoyed the challenge of thinking about how to craft the lessons and what literature to align with the CCSS. For example, we discussed how to use various literary genres such as a graphic novel (a genre that we knew would appeal to students) to meet the CCSS. Lesson components (especially handouts) that we thought were strong to begin with were made all the better because of each other's input. We realized language that was difficult to follow and steps that needed further explication. Vicky's constant questioning about differentiation and meeting the needs of English language learners and struggling learners made Maureen more reflective regarding her classroom approach. Yes, we all want to bring students to a level of success called for by the standards, but how are we addressing the need to provide support for students who may not be ready to meet that level independently just yet? Maureen's passion for providing service learning opportunities to students made Vicky more socially conscious, thereby increasing the social relevance of the lessons.

Answering challenging questions can be frustrating at first. Often, we would find ourselves beginning to provide a rationale for our choices and then interrupting our own chatter and saying, "I'm not even all that sure about this," or, "I'm thinking out loud here; not sure what I want to say." We were each tuned in for the possible, brief, logical, sensible thought that might be mixed in with much of our partner's verbal ruminating. When this happened, we would stop our partner and ask her to repeat herself. This was always validating because we sensed that we had said or heard something of value. At times, it seemed as if we spoke two different languages. In the end, we established a common language, even finishing each other's sentences. This is the beauty of working with a partner.

To return to Ginott, another theorist quoted in this book, we must say that we do believe the experience of collaboration helped us teach to become more humane. We were considerate of one another. We shared in each other's frustrations, provided encouragement when direly needed, and kindly but firmly pushed each other to think at a higher level. It was good for us to experience all of this because this is what we ask our own students to do when they work together.

Here are a few tips on teacher collaboration that we learned along the way of working together on this book:

1. Engage in *co*-labor. This is a partnership—work together not independently. Make shared decisions and assume equal responsibility.

2. Be committed. It is not enough that you share common goals; you also need to be equally committed to the work.

3. Be patient and flexible. Working successfully with others involves patience and understanding. It also involves being open to your collaborator's suggestions and willing to adopt new ideas.

4. Push but gently, and be supportive. Encourage your collaborator to do better through gentle pushing and constant support (by listening, praising, affirming, etc.).

5. Communicate effectively. Clearly articulate your frustrations, questions, and issues regarding the work. Listen to what he or she has to say. Work together to problem-solve.

6. Keep the goal in mind. If the ultimate goal is student success (the objective being effective lessons), then make sure that you keep it in mind throughout the process. Nothing else matters, not even your own ego.

7. Enjoy the process. Reap the benefits of the collaboration (such as introspection, professional growth, improved work product, personal satisfaction, and established collegial relationship).

COLLABORATION WITH OTHER ELA TEACHERS AND OTHER SUBJECT-AREA TEACHERS

Most teachers are naturally social beings. It makes sense for us to collaborate with our colleagues in order to better our approach to teaching. Just as we described above about how working with one another helped to push us to be more introspective about our choices and to enhance our lessons, we have found that within our own schools, interacting with fellow English teachers has had the same effect. We are incredibly grateful to the many colleagues who have helped to shape our career. From insight regarding content and reasonable expectations to managing the paper-load to dealing with stress to celebrating successes, our colleagues have been steady companions, friends, counselors, and cheerleaders.

Of course, when we think about collaboration, we think about collaborating with fellow English teachers, but we must also be mindful of the benefits of working with teachers from outside our beloved subject area. Our students stretch their minds among seven to nine different subjects on any given day. We must try to do the same thing in order to help them make stronger connections to the material they are learning and in order to help ourselves develop a more well-rounded view of content. Working with other content-area teachers to design interdisciplinary lessons allows us recognize the interrelatedness and applicability of what we teach on a daily basis. Picture an English teacher and a social studies teacher collaborating on the Nazi Holocaust. Both teachers want students to understand the causes and impact of World War II and question if war is inevitable or not. In the social studies class, students read primary and secondary sources and discuss events and people involved in the war; in the English class, they read and analyze texts such as *The Diary of Anne Frank*, Elie Wiesel's *Night*, and Jane Yolen's *The Devil's Arithmetic* to understand the human experience of the war. Students in both classes analyze how different writers present varied perspectives regarding the Holocaust. Collaboration is supported by the CCSS's interdisciplinary approach to literacy, which was motivated by the need in college and career for students to be able to read and understand informational texts across the content areas.

The interdependence of the disciplines is evident but needs to be made explicit for students. Succeeding in the discipline of chemistry requires knowledge of mathematics; mastering the Spanish language is facilitated by knowledge of English as the two languages share similarities (e.g., cognates). Through interdisciplinary lessons, students gain not only content knowledge but also analytical and problem-solving skills that they can use across the disciplines. In the Internet era in which we live today, careers require knowledge and awareness of geography, politics, economics as well as culture on a global scale. Large corporations look for employees who have or can access knowledge across disciplines. Being a well-rounded individual gives students a competitive advantage in the workplace and in life.

Teaching in a bubble or teaching with the door closed is no longer an option in a world that is so intensely connected. Just as airplanes and high-speed trains have made travel between what used to be far-off places fast and accessible to the masses, computers and high-speed Internet have decreased the metaphorical distance that students have to travel to make connections among the types of information that they are absorbing in school and out. If we can help them connect what they are learning with us in English to what they are experiencing in another class, there is that much more of a chance of it "sticking."

We mentioned at the beginning of this book that the CCSS for ELA have aligned with the National Assessment of Educational Progress in requiring that 70% of 12th graders' reading be informational. Collaborating with content-area teachers will help to make this informational reading more meaningful. Using service learning along with literacy instruction to construct the bridge that connects content-area teachers' subject matter makes learning more meaningful and more purposeful, and therefore even more likely to be retained by students. For example, English teachers and science teachers join forces to develop a service-learning experience with their students involving tree planting at a local environmental center. Students read an article about the importance of trees written by Nobel Prize winner Wangari Maathai who fought to maintain trees in Kenya. They also analyze the poem "Trees" by Maya Angelou. With a greater understanding of the importance of trees from their science background and their reading in English, they are more invested in planting. This is not just a field trip. This is an extension of classroom learning. Of course, during the planting, students are meeting Speaking and Listening Standards. Upon returning home from this experience, students take part in a reflection activity in which they create collages of photos representing their day. They include statistics and quotes from their prior reading that support the importance of the activity in which they were involved. These posters are displayed to the community so students are motivated to produce a quality product in order to convey their message regarding the importance of maintaining our ecosystem through efforts like theirs. The partnering of two subjects to meet a need and contribute to the common good of the community also meets the common core!

Another example of service learning as an effective means of teacher collaboration is your local toy drive. During the holidays, many schools host a toy drive for families in need. English classes and math classes can join forces to more strategically plan and conduct a toy drive. Students can consider how many families are involved and the makeup of each family. Given the number of children and the number of adults, students can project how much money they would like to spend per child and how much they would like to spend per adult. Also, they may wish to include money for a grocery store gift card. This leads to setting up math equations in order to plan how much money needs to be collected in total and how much to allot per family. Students can budget their money, make preliminary lists through online shopping, and search for coupons and determine how that affects their budgets. Once a budget is set, students can create flyers or proposals to share with the community with a well-developed plan for their toy drive. This is much more sophisticated than putting a box in the lobby and hoping for donations. Add in some literature like

Fly Away Home (a picture book by Eve Bunting about a boy and his father who live in the airport) or a nonfiction piece like Charles M. Blow's *New York Times* piece on the rise in the percentage of children in America who live in low-income homes (2010; see www.nytimes.com/2010/12/25/opinion/25blow .html), and the toy drive takes on even greater meaning both in terms of students' academic growth and social development.

In the following segment, we will discuss the benefits of technology for joining teachers from across town, state, or country. Some of the simplest ways to stay connected include creating shared documents (either in Google.docs or dropbox.com when operating outside of your school or district's network or in a simple shared folder when in the same network). Though, of course, we value face-to-face interaction and support, we recognize that often schedules do not allow for this as frequently as we would like. Working on a shared document allows for teachers who are teaming to work together even when their schedules are not aligned. Please just promise us that you will eventually find some time for lunch or an after-school get-together so that you can have an actual conversation about what you are creating!

COLLABORATION BEYOND THE SCHOOL WALLS

The idea of connecting through organizations and conferences is especially important to us because it advances our professional development. There are several international and national organizations that offer a variety of opportunities for collaboration, including the ASCD (formerly the Association for Supervision and Curriculum Development; www.ascd.org); Association for Middle Level Education (www.nmsa,org); International Reading Association (IRA; www.reading.org); and National Council of Teachers of English (NCTE; www.ncte.org). These associations offer opportunities for members to share and receive resources for improving the teaching of English. Members can participate in advocacy and volunteer forums, publish their ideas and work, and chat online (see more in the *Collaboration in Cyberspace* section below).

Each organization has state and local affiliates or chapters. For example, in New York, there is the New York State English Council (www.nysecteach.org), New York State Reading Association (www.nysra.org), and New York State ASCD (www.newyorkstateascd.org). Members can also apply to form their affiliation, which provides a forum for the exchange of effective instructional practices; affiliates work collaboratively to improve the educational experiences of students worldwide.

ELA Advisory Boards can offer meaningful opportunities for collaboration. Vicky founded the ELA Advisory Board at Molloy College. This board brings together the college's teacher educators and local teachers and administrators for the purpose of exchanging information and knowledge regarding availability of resources to meet the needs of ELA students and educators in community school districts. Members discuss ELA issues (e.g., technology, assessment) and work together to find ways to address them. One way is by offering professional development on topics of interest to preservice and inservice teachers. Similarly, all of the above international organizations offer professional training through conventions, conferences, workshops, institutes, seminars, meetings, and events both offline and online (see the following section for online opportunities).

Each of us has had excellent experiences (and not so excellent) attending ELA conferences. Some simple tips for making the most of your conference experience are as follows:

1. Be prepared—Plan ahead. Take time to review workshop descriptions ahead of time so that you are not giving partial attention to an excellent keynote while trying to plot out your day.

2. Honesty is the best policy—Be honest with yourself. If you are in a workshop that is not what you thought it would be for one reason or another, it is OK to leave (quietly and respectfully, of course). Your time is valuable, and it is likely that there is another workshop that will better meet your needs. Just wait until after you leave to look it up!

3. Plug in—More and more conferences are going paperless. Be sure to be prepared by downloading handouts for sessions that are of interest to you. Doing so will give you a better sense of the workshop itself and help you make a more informed decision as to whether to attend.

4. OMG, your tech is showing!—The fact that many conferences are going paperless does not mean that all speakers will be comfortable with you using your laptop or handheld. Be considerate. Be aware of whether or not the presenter encourages taking notes on your laptop or tweeting about this great speaker as he or she is speaking. Make sure you are not committing a tech faux pas.

5. Just do it—Take matters into your own hands and apply to present at conferences or write for a professional journal. You have a story to tell. You have skills and ideas to share. Just do it!

COLLABORATION IN CYBERSPACE

There's a reason it's called the Web. Consider a spider's web. There are thin lines of thread woven together to form a strong device that captures creatures. In that same sense, individual sites on the Internet weave together to form a strong hub that captures readers' minds. How often have you tried to go online to quickly gather information and then found yourself still on your computer an hour later? You were caught in the Web! Most sites are interconnected. When you look at a website, you can most likely click on a Facebook or Twitter link or click on links to additional related pages. This wealth of information is beneficial, but at times, it can be overwhelming. In the following section, we help you to navigate social networking sites, Internet resources, Web tools, and valuable websites, so that rather than feeling caught in the web, you can put yourself in the role of the spider, weaving together your own powerful hub of sites, resources, and tools.

Social Networking Sites

The following is a list of social networking sites that allow for collaboration. Although these sites are used by the general population, with each site, you can form and find communities around similar interests.

1. **Facebook** (www.Facebook.com) (founded in 2004) is currently the number-one social networking service in the United States that allows people to share information and connect with others.

   - Applications:

     o Share curricular and lesson ideas/plans, best instructional practices, and information regarding current ELA issues with your friends.

     o Create your own group of people with whom you share common interests (e.g., CCSS in ELA).

     o Create and share favorite documents (e.g., ELA lessons, news, and trends) through Facebook (see http://docs.com/).

2. **LinkedIn** (www.LinkedIn.com) (launched in 2003) is currently the world's largest professional network on the Internet. Unlike Facebook, which connects friends (friends, family, colleagues), LinkedIn is a social network mainly for professionals.

   - Applications:

     o Share information and discuss common issues and best practices in the field of ELA. Create groups based on common interests.

     o Use LinkedIn applications to connect with your network. For example, you can use Blog Link to connect your blogs to your profiles.

3. **Twitter** (www.twitter.com) (launched in 2006) is a social networking tool that is based on brevity. All posts or tweets must be 140 characters or fewer. These shot bursts of information can be very powerful. Followers sign up to receive tweets that relate to a topic of interest.

   - Applications:

     o Follow Twitter feeds of authors or politicians and discuss developments with your students.

     o Set up a Twitter account for fellow teachers to keep in contact regarding school issues, or concerns.

     o Set up a Twitter account for your classroom. Have students tweet reactions during presentations. Post live streaming feed on your interactive whiteboard.

     o Get involved with one of Twitter's causes (see www.hope140.org).

4. **NING** (www.ning.com) allows members to create their own networking website. For example, Jim Burke's English Companion (www.english-companion.ning.com) is an exceptional website where ELA teachers can go to ask questions and receive answers.

- Applications:

  o Share and receive information with colleagues through forums, blogs, and interest-based groups, like the groups "Teaching Writing," "Teaching Texts," "Teaching With Blogs and Wikis" created in the English Companion Ning.

  o Create a Ning for your classroom where you and your students can share content.

  o Use Ning applications to enhance your Ning experience. For example, share live content online through Ustream or collaborate and vote on ideas through Ideas or Opinion.

  o With Polldaddy, you can create your own poll and display it for your colleagues or students.

Internet Resources

The following is a list of modes of electronic communication. In this electronic age, we realize that e-mail is a common mode of communication and listservs are becoming more and more popular. A listserv is an electronic mailing list by which members of a group can send and receive e-mail related to a shared topic of interest.

1. **E-mail.** Communicate messages regarding the field of ELA through electronic mail or instant messaging.

2. **Listservs.** The following is a list of tips for making the most of your listserv:

   - **Scan e-mail subject lines.** Choose what to open based on what stands out as connected to your current classroom topics or time-sensitive in terms of testing, politics, current events.

   - **Save e-mails in a folder.** This way, you can do a quick search of subject lines when you want more information on a topic (e.g., search subject lines by *The Scarlet Letter* when you begin a unit on that book).

   - **Decide who you admire.** Develop a sense of whose input is most valuable to you.

   - **Practice proper etiquette.** Contact others offline for materials or to respond personally. Do not reply to the entire listserv community.

   - **Contribute.** Make your listserv what you want it to be. Contribute your information. Respond to others.

3. **Web Tools**

   Blogs—Web logs usually based on a particular topic. Many teachers have taken to blogging about issues in education. The professional sites listed below have links to several blogs.

   - Applications:

     o Set up your own blog to discuss happenings in your school or in the greater community concerning education.

     o Create or contribute to an existing blog for discussing literature or lesson ideas with other teachers.

    ○ Have students create blogs based on content that you are covering in class.

Podcasts (or webcasts)—Audio or visual episodes that can be downloaded for listening or viewing.

- Applications:

    ○ View or listen to podcasts to increase your own content knowledge.

    ○ Select appropriate podcasts of use in your classroom (see more under Tedtalks in the websites section below).

Wikis—Webpages that can be edited by its users (wikispaces.com).

- Applications:

    ○ Create a wiki for other teachers and share content (for example, lessons on teaching writing). You can write and edit these lessons and share them.

    ○ Create a wiki for your classroom using the K–12 wiki plan. With a wiki, you and your students can share text, images, and files. Students can publish their work on the wiki. You can also embed video, audio, and images to enhance your multimedia assignments. You can create student accounts that do not require e-mail addresses.

Google.docs, dropbox.com, and Microsoft Office Live Workplace— Applications that allow the viewing of documents on the Internet.

- Applications:

    ○ Share your personal work with other teachers or collaborate on a project together.

Valuable Websites

The following is a list of 20 websites that we have found especially useful. Some of these sites are helpful for developing lesson plans. Many of the sites offer teacher-created lesson plans. Like the lessons in this book, these lessons are valuable because they have been tried and tested in the classroom. These sites allow for collaboration with teachers near and far who post their successful lessons. Other sites offer expert information from journalists, scientists, historians, and so on. This is the beauty of the Web. Most of us would never have the opportunity to collaborate with such experts if not for the Internet. Other websites offer far more than just learning resources; they open a door to educational communities (i.e., research, online discussions, opportunities for advocacy and face-to-face interactions at conferences, workshops, and meetings).

    1. ASCD (www.ascd.org)

    What we like about it . . .

- ASCDEdge—a professional networking community for educators that is similar to Facebook, but includes only people in education.

- ASCD Professional Interest Communities—member-initiated groups designed to unite people around a common area of interest in the field of education.
- ASCD Connected Communities—defined by geographic boundaries and help bring together groups of individuals concerned with improving teaching and learning.
- Links to publications including *Education Leadership* and *Educational Update* along with full-length books.

2. **Association for Middle Level Education** (www.nmsa.org) (formerly National Middle School Association)

What we like about it . . .

- Offers a MiddleTalk listserv.
- Suggests advocacy opportunities.
- Provides links to publications, including *Middle School Journal* and *Middle Ground* along with full-length books.

3. **Bibliomania** (www.bibliomania.com)

This site contains thousands of literary works, including books, articles, short stories, and poems. Also posted are literary research, reference materials, biographies, nonfiction, and some religious texts.

What we like about it . . .

- If you register (for free), you gain access to study guides and you can share questions or comments by posting them on a message board for fellow readers to see.
- The site has a link for sharing teacher resources.
- Shopping! This site reviews thousands of books, arranges selected titles by theme, and offers the books at a discounted price.

4. **Brainpop** (www.brainpop.com)

This site offers a variety of content areas to choose from and seems to cover almost every topic under a content area with numerous examples, facts, and ideas. The site is also student-centered with its fun coloring and engaging organization.

What we like about it . . .

- Students will like the explanatory videos, but some are a bit basic for more mature students.
- Brainpop Educators allows you to access lesson plans by grade level and subject area. At this time, the site has more than 135,000 members and 850 free resources.

5. **Colorín Colorado** (www.colorincolorado.org)

This is a site that is a product of a collaboration between Reading Rockets and the American Federation of Teachers. It is a bilingual

(English and Spanish) site that offers useful information, strategies, and activities for teachers of English language learners (ELLs) as well as content teachers who have ELLs in their classes. However, many of the strategies suggested are applicable to all students, no matter what their primary language. With a growing number of ELLs in the United States, the site offers helpful resources to address the challenge of teaching English to diverse students. The site states that even though the activities have been designed for preK to Grade 3 students, most can be adapted for students in Grades 4–12.

What we like about it . . .

- The toolkits for educators (i.e., Toolkit for teachers: Reaching Out to Hispanic Parents of ELLs; ELL Starter Kit for Educators; Reading Tip Sheets for ELL Educators) are important resources that every teacher should have.
- A wealth of information is offered regarding reaching out to Hispanic students and families (Spanish-speakers comprise more than 70% of ELLs in the United States).
- Resources for ELLs are divided by grade or topic.
- Video and podcasts about various topics are available.

6. Complete Works of William Shakespeare (http://shakespeare.mit .edu/works.html)

A complete guide to Shakespeare. There is information on each play with a small biography on Shakespeare. All of the exact texts are given online.

What we like about it . . .

- Availability of full text to cut and paste sections for analysis when designing handouts.

7. Discover Education (http://school.discoveryeducation.com)

Teacher-centered site with lesson plans and activities to give to students. The site is run by the Discovery Channel.

What we like about it . . .

- Adaptable literature-based and skills-based lesson plans under Teachers, 9–12, English.
- Also, check out the lesson plans in other subject areas and consider opportunities for interdisciplinary planning.
- Kathy Schrock's *Guide for Educators* has an excellent research support guide.
- English Homework Help under the Student section provides links to sites in Writing, Mechanics, and Grammar.

8. Edufind.com (www.edufind.com)

This site has useful sections broken down based on teaching grammar. It provides activities and lessons.

What we like about it . . .

- Free tests to assess students' language capability.
- Interactive games to improve language skills.
- Grammar Q&A includes video and/or audio responses along with useful links for further information.
- Extensive list of grammar categories ranging from types of words to usage to writing and much more.

9. **Folger Shakespeare Library** (www.folger.edu)

This site is based on the concept of performance-based teaching (PBT). According to Folger, this means "an interactive approach to the study of literature, particularly Shakespeare's plays and poems, in which students participate in a close reading of text through intellectual, physical, and vocal engagement." The site offers lesson plans, study guides, and videos related to PBT. They also produce a monthly newsletter call *Bardnotes* and maintain a blog with teacher information such as upcoming performances, workshops, and institutes.

What we like about it . . .

- Opportunities to interact with fellow teachers and experts at institutes, conferences, and through webinars.
- Study guides with research-based information and classic artwork.
- Teacher to teacher—short videos of teachers sharing their tips for sharing Shakespeare with students. Each video is accompanied by a lesson plan.

10. **Go to Service Learning** (http://gotoservicelearning.org)

This site provides teacher-developed service learning lessons sorted by content, themes, grade level, target populations, duration, setting, and place of impact.

What we like about it . . .

- Finding lessons that fit your needs is extremely easy because of the parameters by which you can narrow your search.
- The common template for all lessons makes for a wealth of information from Essential Questions, Service-Learning Themes, Curriculum Connections, Stages of Service Learning, Assessment and Evaluation.

11. **In Our Global Village** (www.inourvillage.org)

This site provides the background on the first *In Our Village* book, published by students in a small village in Tanzania. The efforts of these students to support themselves by sharing their story with the world have resulted in more than 20 *In Our Village* books written by students from all over the world—from California to Pennsylvania, to Estonia, to India. This is collaboration at its best—teachers and students develop related work from all over the globe!

What we like about it . . .

- Offers multiple approaches and models (thematic chapters, narratives of residents, focus on a particular aspect of the area such as the birds of Tanzania) for telling the stories of students' experiences.
- Students may also help tell the story of foreign places (i.e., *In Our Village Darfur* was written by students in Estonia).
- Provides a meaningful venue for publishing student work.
- Videos links of students in Tanzania.

12. **International Reading Association's Engage** (http://engage.reading.org)

What we like about it . . .

- Helps literacy professionals expand their professional relations by offering opportunities to create a community or a blog and list events on the online community.

13. **National Council of Teachers of English Connected Community** (http://ncte.connectedcommunity.org)

What we like about it . . .

- Allows members to connect through discussions, blogs, and online groups (i.e., topical, affiliate, constituent).
- Features Readwritethink.org, a site that offers excellent lesson plans, teacher videos, booklists, and more.

14. **National Public Radio** (www.npr.org)

This site includes a vast collection on nonfiction in written and audio form.

What we like about it . . .

- *This American Life*—described in *This American Life* lesson plan
- Storycorps—this is a venue for recording stories about loved ones that might otherwise be lost.
- Picture Show—this page includes stunning photos that are ripe for analysis. Students can apply the skills they use to analyze the photos to analyzing text.

15. **Poetry Foundation** (www.poetryfoundation.org)

This is a site that discovers and celebrates poetry.

What we like about it . . .

- Includes a learning lab that offers learning resources on select poems (including writing ideas, discussion questions, teaching tips, etc.).
- Offers numerous resources, such as articles about poetry, essays on poetic theory, and glossary of poetic terms.

16. **Public Broadcasting Service Teachers** (www.pbs.org/teachers)

PBS Teachers provides preK–12 educational resources, including lesson plans, classroom teaching activities, on-demand videos, and interactive games.

What we like about it . . .

- Thousands of classroom resources are available that are suitable for a wide range of subjects and grade levels.
- Resources are broken down according to grade level, subject, media type, and PBS programming.
- These resources are tied to PBS's on-air and online programming (e.g., *NOVA, Nature*), allowing for multiple opportunities for multimedia assignments.
- Offers video products on education topics.
- Educators may participate in online discussions and blogs.

17. **Technology Entertainment Design (TED)** (www.ted.com/)

The tagline for this site is "riveting talks by remarkable people, free to the world." Whether you are looking to develop a basic understanding of a topic that is foreign to you or to learn more about a topic that is familiar to you, this is a great resource. Videos are under 20 minutes, so viewers remain engaged in the talk.

What we like about it . . .

- Information is organized according to theme and interest level (most viewed, most e-mailed, "jaw-dropping," etc.).
- Interactive opportunities through blogging and through Ted Conversations. This link allows users to post questions, comments, or debates. Other users then respond.
- Translations of talks are available.

18. **This I Believe** (www.thisibelieve.org)

This site is an archive of more than 90,000 essays written around the theme of core values or beliefs. Many are available as podcasts. In addition, the site offers grade level appropriate curriculum guides for infusing This I Believe in your curriculum.

What we like about it . . .

- Podcasts for use when practicing listening and note-taking skills.
- Curriculum guides.
- A forum for publishing essays.
- You may even be able to get the executive producer of This I Believe to visit your school!

19. **Web English Teacher** (www.webenglishteacher.com)

This site for English teachers covers numerous topics including strategies for ELLs, advanced placement students, and many literacy strategies specific to English teachers.

What we like about it . . .

- Offers valuable Web links to information, lesson plans, activities, videos, criticism, tests and quizzes on various ELA topics, including teaching with technology, mythology, poetry, grammar, and Shakespeare.
- Provides a wealth of information—The list of websites seems endless.

20. **WLIW21** (www.wliw.org)

The site offers a wide selection of resources including a section for educators with Regents review. Teachers must create an account to continuously view information; however, seven resources can be viewed during a "test drive" session.

What we like about it . . .

- Lessons are categorized by Reading and Viewing or Writing and Speaking.
- Subcategories of reading include Genres, Reading Fundamentals, Text Comprehension Skills, and Visual Media Skills.
- Subcategories of writing include Research, Style and Rhetoric, and The Writing Process.
- Videos of poets and authors reading their work.
- Many of the lessons are interactive and self-paced on the computer, but this means that students have to sign-in.

CONCLUSION

Collaboration today looks different from collaboration of the past. No longer are we confined within our school walls when it comes to seeking advice or input from a colleague. Rather, technology has raised the roof off of the schoolhouse, allowing us to collaborate with people outside of our buildings, town, state, and even nation. The sites and tools that we have listed are our favorites. We are sure that you have favorites of your own. Remember, collaboration means *working together.* One simple way for you to work together with us is to access the handouts for the lessons within this book and adapt them to suit your needs. The handouts are available at www.corwinpress.com.

Though you are reaching the final pages of this book, your experience with the Common Core State Standards for ELA and hopefully your work with us is just beginning. We hope that by reading this book, you have come closer to the core of these standards and that the lessons will help you create some effective learning experiences for your students. Earlier in this book, based on Wiggins and McTighe's metaphor, we indicated we were on the road to effective lesson design with Dewey, Bloom, and Gardner as our backseat drivers. What we did not tell you is that we are driving a big yellow school bus, and we have plenty of room for you. Jump in and we will all enjoy the ride together!

References

Abraham Lincoln's wonderful way with words. (2011, February 4). *Read, 60*(10), 20–21.

Achieve, Inc. (2007). *Closing the expectations gap 2007: An annual 50-state progress report on the alignment of high school policies with the demands of college and work.* Washington, DC: Author. Retrieved from http://www.achieve.org/files/50-state-07-Final.pdf.

ACT, Inc. (2006). *Reading between the lines: What the ACT reveals about college readiness in reading.* Iowa City, IA: Author.

ACT, Inc. (2009a). *ACT national curriculum survey.* Iowa City, IA: Author.

ACT, Inc. (2009b). *The condition of college readiness 2009.* Iowa City, IA: Author.

ACT, Inc. (2010). *A first look at the common core and college and career readiness.* Retrieved from http://www.act.org/research/policymakers/pdf/FirstLook.pdf.

Allen, R. (2003, Summer). Expanding writing's role in learning: Teacher training holds key to change. *Curriculum Update.* Retrieved from http://www.ascd.org/publications/curriculum-update/summer2003/Expanding-Writing's-Role-in-Learning.aspx.

Aronson, M. (2008, October 1). Being and nothingness. *School Library Journal.* Retrieved from http://www.libraryjournal.com/slj/printissue/currentissue/859826-427/being_and_nothingness.html.csp.

Beck, I. L., McKeown, L. L., & Kucan, L. (2002). *Bringing words to life: Robust vocabulary instruction.* New York: Guilford Press.

Birner, B. (n.d.). Is language always changing? *The Linguistics Society of America.* Retrieved from http://www.lsadc.org/info/ling-faqs-change.cfm.

Bloom, B. S. (1956). *Taxonomy of educational objectives, handbook I: The cognitive domain.* New York: David McKay.

Blow, C. M. (2010, December 24). Suffer the little children. *The New York Times.* Retrieved from http://www.nytimes.com/2010/12/25/opinion/25blow.html.

Burke, J. (2010). *What's the big idea? Question-driven units to motivate reading, writing, and thinking.* Portsmouth, NH: Heinemann.

Buss, F. L. (2002). *Journey of the sparrows.* New York: Puffin Books.

Caruso, J. (1999). My life in a bag. *Electronic Magazine of Multicultural Education* [online], *1*(4). Retrieved from http://www.eastern.edu/publications/1999fall/caruso.html.

Cisneros, S. (1991). *The house on Mango Street.* New York: Vintage Books.

Clinton, President W. J. (1997, February 4). [State of the Union Address]. Presented to a joint session of the 105th United States Congress, Washington, DC. Retrieved from http://clinton2.nara.gov/WH/SOU97/.

The Consortium: The Conference Board, Corporate Voices for Working Families, Partnership for 21st Century Skills, Society for Human Resource Management.

(2006). *Are they really ready to work? Employers' perspectives on the basic knowledge and applied skills of new entrants to the 21st century workforce.* Washington, DC: Author.

Cormier, R. (1974). *The chocolate war.* New York: Random House.

The Council of Writing Program Administrators (CWPA), the National Council of Teachers of English (NCTE), and the National Writing Project (NWP). (2011). *Framework for success in postsecondary writing.* Berkeley, CA: NWP.

Crovitz, D., & Miller, J. A. (2008). Register and charge: Using synonym maps to explore connotation. *English Journal, 97*(4), 49–55.

Crystal, D. (2009). *Txtng: The Gr8 Db8.* New York: Oxford University Press.

Dalton, J., & Smith, D. (1986).Extending children's special abilities—Strategies for primary classrooms. *Teachers on the Web: Aussie School House,* 36–37. Retrieved from http://www.teachers.ash.org.au/researchskills/dalton.htm.

DeCosta, M., Clifton, J., & Roen, D. (2010). Collaboration and social interaction in English Classrooms. *English Journal, 99*(5), 14–21.

Dewey, J. (1938). *Experience and education.* New York: Collier Books.

DuFour, R., & Eaker, R. (1998). *Professional learning communities at work: Best practices for enhancing student achievement.* Bloomington, IA: National Education Service.

Dunn, P. A., & Lindblom, K. (2011). *Grammar rants: How a backstage tour of writing complaints can help students make informed, savvy choices about their writing.* Portsmouth, NH: Heinemann/Boynton/Cook.

Felten, P. (2008). Visual literacy. *Change: The Magazine of Higher Learning, 40*(4), 60–64.

Figgins, M. A., & Johnson, J. (2007). Wordplay: The poem's second language. *English Journal, 96*(3), 29–34.

Flynt, E. S., & Brozo, W. (2010). Visual literacy and the content classroom: A question of now, not when. *The Reading Teacher, 63*(6), 526–528.

Futernick, K. (2007). *A possible dream: Retaining California's teachers so all students learn.* Sacramento: California State University.

Gardner, H. (1983). *Frames of mind: The theory of multiple intelligences.* New York: Basic.

Gawron, H. W. (2011).*'Tween crayons and curfews: Tips for middle school teachers.* Larchmont, NY: Eye on Education.

Goddard, Y. L., Goddard, R. D., & Taschannen-Moran, M. (2007). A theoretical and empirical investigation of teacher collaboration for school improvement and student achievement in public elementary schools. *Teachers College Record, 109*(4), 877–896.

Graves, D. (1983). *Writing: teachers and children at work.* Portsmouth, NH: Heinemann.

Kamil, M. L. (2003). *Adolescents and literacy: Reading for the 21st century.* Washington, DC: Alliance for Excellent Education.

Kelley, S. (2010, February 1). Texting, Twitter contributing to students' poor grammar skills, profs say. *The Globe: Canadian Press.* Retrieved from http://www.theglobeandmail.com/news/technology/texting-twitter-contributing-to-students-poor-grammar-skills-profs-say/article1452300/.

Kipp-Newbold, R. (2010). That's fierce! Collaboration in the English classroom. *English Journal, 99*(5), 74–78.

Lindblom, K., & Dunn, P. A. (2006). Analyzing grammar rants: An alternative to traditional grammar instruction. *English Journal, 95*(5), 71–77.

Meyers, G. D. (2002). Whose inquiry is it anyway? Using students' questions in the teaching of literature. In J. Holden & J. S. Schmit (Eds.), *Inquiry and the literary text: Constructing discussions in the English classroom* (pp. 60–71). Urbana, IL: National Council of Teachers of English.

National Center for Education Evaluation and Regional Assistance (NCERA)/The Institute of Education Sciences (IES). (2008). *Turning around chronically low-performing schools.* Washington, DC: U.S. Department of Education. Retrieved from http://ies.ed.gov/ncee/wwc/pdf/practiceguides/Turnaround_pg_04181.pdf.

National Governors Association Center for Best Practices (NGA)/Council of Chief State School Officers (CCSSO). (2010a). *About the standards.* Retrieved from http://www.corestandards.org/about-the-standards.

National Governors Association Center for Best Practices (NGA)/Council of Chief State School Officers (CCSSO). (2010b). *Common Core State Standards for ELA, literacy in history/social studies, science, and technical subjects.* Retrieved from http://www.corestandards.org/assets/CCSSI_ELA%20Standards.pdf.

National Governors Association Center for Best Practices (NGA)/Council of Chief State School Officers (CCSSO). (2010c). *Common Core State Standards for ELA, literacy in history/social studies, science, and technical subjects. Appendix A.* Retrieved from http://www.corestandards.org/assets/Appendix_A.pdf.

National Governors Association Center for Best Practices (NGA)/Council of Chief State School Officers (CCSSO). (2010d). *Common Core State Standards for ELA, literacy in history/social studies, science, and technical subjects. Appendix B.* Retrieved from http://www.corestandards.org/assets/Appendix_B.pdf.

No Child Left Behind Act of 2001, Pub. L. No. 107-110, 115 Stat. 1425 §1001 [Statement of purpose] (2002). Retrieved from http://www2.ed.gov/policy/elsec/leg/esea02/pg1.html.

Norton360online. *Social engineering.* Retrieved from http://www.norton360online.com/security-center/social-engineering.html.

Orwell, G. (1945). *Animal farm.* Orlando, FL: Harcourt Brace & Company.

Oxford word list. (2009). New York: Oxford University Press. Retrieved from http://www.oxfordwordlist.com.

Partnership for 21st Century Skills. (2006). *Most young people entertaining the U.S. workforce lack critical skills essential for success.* Retrieved from http://www.p21.org/index.php?option=com_content&task=view&id=250&Itemid=64.

RAND Reading Study Group. (2002). *Reading for understanding: Toward an R & D program in reading comprehension.* Santa Monica, CA: RAND.

Rothstein, E., & Rothstein, A. S. (2009). *English grammar instruction that works: Developing language skills for all learners.* Thousand Oakes, CA: Corwin.

Ryan, E. (1992). *How to make grammar fun—and easy!* Mahwah, NJ: Troll Associates.

Schmoker, M. (1999). *Results: The key to continuous school improvement* (2nd ed.). Alexandria, VA: Association for Supervision and Curriculum Development.

Skube, M. (2006, August 27). Writing off reading. *Washington Post.* Retrieved from http://www.washingtonpost.com/wp-dyn/content/article/2006/08/18/AR2006081800976.html.

Smith, T. B. (2008). Teaching vocabulary expeditiously: Three keys to improving vocabulary instruction. *English Journal, 97*(4), 20–25.

Soven, M. I. (1999). *Teaching writing in middle and secondary schools: Theory, research, and practice.* Boston, MA: Allyn & Bacon.

Steinbeck, J. (1937). *Of mice and men.* New York: Penguin.

Tan, S. (2006). *The arrival.* New York: Scholastic.

Tomlinson, C. A., & McTighe, J. (2006). *Integrating differentiated instruction and understanding by design.* Alexandria, VA: Association for Supervision and Curriculum Development.

Vygotsky, L. S. (1978). *Mind in society: Development of higher psychological processes.* Cambridge, MA: Harvard University Press.

Weingarten, G. (2010, September 19). Goodbye, cruel words: English. It's dead to me. *The Washington Post.* Retrieved from http://www.washingtonpost.com/wp-dyn/content/article/2010/09/13/AR2010091304476.html.

Wiggins, G. (2010). Why we should stop bashing tests. *Educational Leadership, 67*(6), 48–52.

Wiggins, G., & McTighe, J. (2001). *Understanding by design* (1st ed.). Upper Saddle River, NJ: Merrill Prentice Hall.

Wiggins, G., & McTighe, J. (2005). *Understanding by design* (2nd ed.). Alexandria, VA: Association for Supervision and Curriculum Development.

Appendix

Lesson Plan Template

Lesson Plan Template

TOPIC (GRADE LEVEL):

TEXTS TYPES AND PURPOSES:

CCSS STRAND:

TIMING:

BACKWARD DESIGN COMPONENTS:
DESIRED RESULTS/CCSS ADDRESSED:

SUPPLEMENTAL RESOURCES:

ACCEPTABLE EVIDENCE:

TECHNOLOGY/MEDIA OPPORTUNITIES:

LEARNING EXPERIENCES AND INSTRUCTION:

SERVICE LEARNING LINK:

STRATEGIES (e.g., guidance and monitoring, modeling, cooperative learning, discussion, and writing process):

VARIATIONS:

Index

CORWIN

A SAGE Company

The Corwin logo—a raven striding across an open book—represents the union of courage and learning. Corwin is committed to improving education for all learners by publishing books and other professional development resources for those serving the field of PreK–12 education. By providing practical, hands-on materials, Corwin continues to carry out the promise of its motto: **"Helping Educators Do Their Work Better."**